careers & jobs
in
nursing

Taking the hard work out of finding your dream job!

NurseFinders UK has been in operation for four years and during that time we have helped many qualified, registered nurses find their ideal jobs in the UK. It was set up by nurses who understand the problems of relocating and finding worthwhile career opportunities in the UK. We consider our friendly and professional approach a refreshing change to both candidates and clients alike.

Our website is user friendly and gives essential information with regards to working and living in the UK. We ensure that EVERY nurse that enters their information onto the website has a response within 24 hours of registering.

Our Clients include NHS Trusts, private hospitals, nursing and residential homes and homes for people with learning disabilities and many primary care and nurse advisor organizations all over the UK.

We invite you to visit our website at **www.nursefindersuk.com** for more information about our company. Alternatively you could call us on **01732 355 585** or email us at **careers@nursefindersuk.com**

THE TIMES

careers & jobs
in
nursing

linda nazarko

KOGAN
PAGE

Scottish readers should be aware that, in order to simplify the text, the author has referred only to NVQs. In nearly every respect, these are the same as their Scottish equivalent, SVQs.

Publisher's note
Every possible effort has been made to ensure that the information contained in this book is accurate at the time of going to press, and the publishers and authors cannot accept responsibility for any errors or omissions, however caused. No responsibility for loss or damage occasioned to any person acting, or refraining from action, as a result of the material in this publication can be accepted by the editor, the publisher or the author.

First published in Great Britain in 2004

Kogan Page Limited
120 Pentonville Road
London N1 9JN
United Kingdom
www.kogan-page.co.uk

The views expressed in this book are those of the author, and are not necessarily the same as those of Times Newspapers Ltd.

British Library Cataloguing in Publication Data

A CIP record for this book is available from the British Library.

ISBN 0 7494 4249 2

Typeset by Saxon Graphics Ltd, Derby
Printed and bound in Great Britain by Bell & Bain, Glasgow

Contents

Foreword

I am honoured to have been invited to write the foreword to this edition of Careers and Jobs in Nursing. I have enjoyed tremendous opportunities and challenges throughout my own career in nursing. It is a privilege to have the chance to encourage others to make a career out of caring.

As this book shows, there is a whole range of careers in nursing and many different and rewarding career paths are available. I am particularly enthusiastic about the way that entry to nursing has become more accessible in recent years. This really is changing the face of nursing and the profile of the nursing workforce, because there are more varied opportunities than ever before to get into nursing.

The Royal College of Nursing (RCN) is strongly committed to the future of nursing as a graduate profession, but with a whole variety of ways into nursing education. Many people now start on nursing courses having gained valuable – and transferable – experience and education during their time as health care assistants. There is a choice of degree and diploma courses on offer, and many nursing students today combine their studies and clinical placements with caring for family members. It is possible to work in, for example, hospitals, GP surgeries, clinics, nursing and residential homes, occupational health services, voluntary organisations that run hospices or residential care and the pharmaceutical industry. Nurses also work in the prison service, university education, on leisure cruise ships or for the armed forces. Many nurses spend a year or two gaining professional experience outside the UK.

Nurses focus on the needs of the individual, rather than specific, illnesses or conditions. They help individuals and their families to live more comfortable lives by providing care, advice and counselling. No two patients are the same, and every working day is different.

Nursing requires the ability to work in a team, to think on your feet and to have excellent communication skills. You will be accountable for your actions and their consequences and you need to have a passion for lifelong learning; I have been in clinical practice for many years and I am now studying for a doctorate. It's not about having letters after one's name; it's about the quest for new knowledge and understanding to help enrich the body of nursing knowledge and translate it into improved patient care. Nursing requires you, above all, to shape and deliver care that is scientifically sound, but which responds to patients' essential humanity, and which does so in a way that connects, rather than mechanising and alienating. It takes nursing leadership at all levels, be it the bedside, the boardroom or the patient's home, to make it a reality.

As nurses, the people and communities we care for are increasingly diverse. I fully support the moves to make sure that the nursing team reflects that diversity. Age, gender, spirituality, sexuality and ethnicity are all strengths, not weaknesses. The stereotype of the nursing student as a young, white, single female is long gone – and so is the stereotype of our patients and clients as passive recipients of care. Today, nurses are forging partnerships of mutual respect with patients. Changes in society, demography and technological advances have made health care one of the most exciting, complex and challenging areas of life. Nurses have a vital part in proactive healthcare, moving away from a sickness towards a health service. As nurses we know that people need and want high quality, easily accessible care; they also need the help of trusted professionals to make meaningful choices.

Nursing is a profession that works closely with patients, carers, service users and the general public on a day by day basis, and often over long periods of time. Nurses are ideally placed to help patients access and understand reliable information in order to make important choices about the care and treatment they want. To do this we have to be able to recruit and retain nurses – which is why it is essential that the new pay and career package for nurses, Agenda for Change, is implemented successfully.

I commend this book to you as an excellent introduction to careers in nursing and I hope that it will inform and inspire you to come into the profession yourself.

Sylvia Denton OBE FRCN
President of the Royal College of Nursing

Introduction

NURSING AS A CAREER

Nursing is a career that many people find attractive. Last year over 87,000 people applied for nurse education programmes, 15,000 were successful in gaining places. Many people say 'I'd love to be a nurse but ...'. People sometimes think that they have left it too late to become a nurse or that they do not have the qualifications or that they would not be considered for some other reason. This book aims to give you up-to-date information about the different types of nursing, what type of people are accepted to become nurses, what qualifications are needed and how to obtain them.

Is nursing the career for you?

Nursing is an exciting, interesting and broad profession where no two days' work are the same. Nurse education is the first step on the career ladder within nursing. Students learn about anatomy, physiology, disease processes and how illness affects a person. They learn about health promotion and helping people with chronic diseases such as diabetes to remain well. Nursing is a practical profession and throughout your education programme you will have clinical placements. On a clinical placement you will learn the practice of nursing. In university you will be taught nursing skills and will often use anatomical models for practice. On your placements you will observe, practise and perfect those skills with real patients. Nurse education is 50 per cent university-based and 50 per cent practice-based.

Use the checklist below to see whether nursing is the career for you.

	Yes	No
Do you enjoy working with people?		
Do you wish to help people to recover from illness?		
Do you have a caring nature?		
Do you enjoy helping people to work out problems?		
Can you work well as part of a team?		
Could you lead a team?		
Are you enthusiastic and keen to become a nurse?		
Are you a good listener?		
Do you care about people?		
Do you want a job where you want to make a real difference to people's lives?		

The most important attribute that a nurse must have is the right attitude or approach. This means having the ability to put yourself in the sick person's place, to understand how the person is feeling and to have the ability to work with that person. Technical skills can be learnt during your education programme and throughout your career.

What type of people become nurses

Many people think that nursing is a career for young single women who enter the profession straight out of school. That image is now out of date – 46 per cent of those entering the profession are over 25 years old. Furthermore, although nursing remains a female dominated profession, 12 per cent of student nurses are male.

People enter nurse education at different times in their lives. Some people start off working as a health care assistant and decide to become a nurse. Some people have other careers but find them unsatisfying and decide to become a nurse. Some women who have raised a family decide to enter nursing when their children are older. The oldest student nurse in the

UK is 55 and many people in their 40s and 50s have decided to become nurses.

Where do people nurse?

As a registered nurse you can choose to work in a variety of settings including, hospitals, GP surgeries, nurse-led walk-in centres and minor injury units, nursing and residential homes, occupational health services, and the pharmaceutical industry. You can also work as a nurse teacher in a university or hospital, in the prison service, on cruise ships or for the armed forces.

The NHS employs 73 per cent of all nurses. However, the number of nurses working in other settings has increased dramatically in recent years – 3 per cent work as practice nurses; 11 per cent work in nursing homes and 13 per cent work in private hospitals – and these numbers continue to grow.

Nursing within the NHS is varied. Nurses work either in hospitals or in the community. In the past most nursing was concentrated in hospitals but this is changing. The government realises that if we are to keep people well we need to have more nurses working with people outside hospitals. There are now increasing numbers of community nurses.

Nurses work in different specialities (see Chapter 1 for details). NHS nurses working in community and hospital settings make up the majority with approximately 180,000 working in general nursing. However, 40,000 nurses work within psychiatric care, approximately 8,000 work within children's nursing, 4,000 as learning disability nurses and approximately 50,000 within community nursing.

CAREER PATHWAYS

Nursing has moved a long way in recent years. Registered nurses once worked as staff nurses and those who were promoted to sister or charge nurse posts had to move into management or education if they wished to gain further promotion. That has now changed. Now nurses who wish to can develop a career in clinical practice. They can become nurse specialists or nurse consultants. Figure 0.1, taken from the Department of Health's work on nursing careers, shows four stages in career progression. The nurse is required to gain additional skills in order to progress through the pathway.

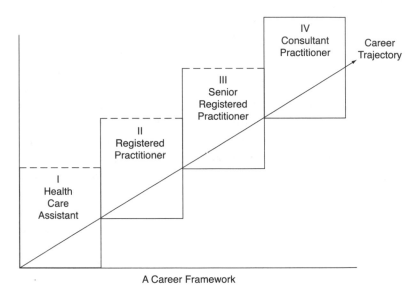

A Career Framework

Figure 0.1

TOP TIPS FOR GETTING A NURSING PLACE

The number of people applying to join nurse education programmes is rising nationally. As the number of applicants rises competition for places becomes more intense. If you wish to become a nurse you can increase your chances of success by reading this book and learning as much as you can about nursing and by following these top tips.

TOP TIPS

If you are still at school:

■ Work hard and get the best grades you can.

■ Get some work experience in nursing settings. This will help you to find out what nursing is really like and if you do want to be a nurse.

■ Talk to your careers adviser and obtain information. Many schools have careers sessions where people from different professions visit the school and talk to students about careers.

If you are working as a care assistant and do not have entry qualifications consider obtaining an NVQ level qualification. These provide nursing entry qualifications.

If you do not have entry qualifications consider an access to nursing course at college. Enquire if the college has pre-course resources to help applicants, such as aids to improve numeracy skills (see the Appendix page 116).

If you are working as a care assistant in the NHS and have entry qualifications enquire about sponsored places.

If you are working full-time in a non-health care setting consider working as a volunteer in your local hospital or nursing home. This will give you some insight into nursing.

Read the popular nursing journals to find out about nursing. You can buy *Nursing Times* and *Nursing Standard* from large newsagents. You can also find out about nursing using the Internet, see Chapter 10 for further information.

Types of nursing

1

This chapter aims to provide information about nurse education programmes and how they are structured. It also gives information about the four branches of nursing in which you can specialise as a student.

NURSE EDUCATION PROGRAMMES

In the UK the Nursing and Midwifery Council (NMC) regulates nursing. All nurse educational programmes must meet NMC standards. One stipulation is that nurse education programmes must have 4,600 hours of study. These hours are delivered through a three-year programme consisting of 50 per cent theory and 50 per cent practice.

The first year of the programme is known as the common foundation course. During the common foundation course students learn skills that are applicable to all branches of nursing. In the second and third years students specialise in a particular branch of nursing. There are four branches of nursing:

- adult nursing;
- children's nursing;
- learning disability nursing;
- mental health nursing.

Students are normally expected to specify which branch they wish to specialise in before they begin their nursing education. Few universities offer students the opportunity to decide on which branch programme they wish to follow during the common foundation course. All universities have contracts with the NHS to educate specific numbers of students for each branch of nursing. The universities need to know which branch students are applying for so that they can meet their contracts and educate the appropriate number of students on each branch programme. Students who, having already opted for one branch of nursing, discover that they really want to specialise in a different branch may be able to change their course of study. Universities have a formal process for this. No university will guarantee that a student can change branches but most will do their best to help a student in this situation.

All nursing students must follow a programme that has the following components:

- professional, ethical and legal issues;

- the theory and practice of nursing;

- the context in which health and social care is delivered;

- organisational structures and processes;

- communication;

- social and life sciences relevant to nursing practice;

- frameworks for social care provision and care systems.

In the first year of their nursing education programme students learn theory and develop skills that are common to all branches. In the second and third years students learn theory and develop skills that are specific to the branch they are studying. The student studying on the children's nursing branch will learn about communication in the context of children and their families.

Students are required to obtain core competencies at different levels throughout their programme. These skills are gained in the workplace and assessed by registered nurses.

Students are also required to complete academic assignments to demonstrate that they understand and can apply nursing theory to practice.

· When students have successfully completed their educational programme they are able to register as nurses. The minimum standard for nurse registration is now diploma level, but growing numbers of nurses now obtain a degree in nursing and there are Master's degree programmes available. You will find more details in Chapter 2.

ADULT NURSING

Adult nursing is the most popular branch of nursing and most students choose to specialise in adult nursing.

THE ROLE OF THE ADULT NURSE

- Assess care needs and work with the person to develop a plan of care.

- Deliver care if the person is unable to care for him- or herself.

- Enable the person to regain independence following illness or injury.

- Support the person and his or her family during illness or after an accident.

- Monitor the effectiveness of treatment.

Some nurses who specialise in adult nursing go on to obtain further qualifications in other branches of nursing. Of these, many go on to obtain further qualifications in midwifery (see Chapter 3) or community nursing (see Chapter 7). Some nurses choose to specialise in a particular area of practice within their chosen branch. The nurse who has registered as an adult nurse may choose to specialise in care of older people, or accident and emergency nursing.

Students who choose to specialise in adult nursing have placements in hospital and community settings. In hospitals the student would work on medical and surgical wards, in the operating theatre, intensive care, accident and emergency departments and gain some experience in children's wards. Students also spend time with registered midwives looking after mothers and newborn babies.

In the community students work with district nurses visiting people at home and delivering care. The student may also be able to attend a specialist clinic, such as a leg ulcer clinic run by a district nurse. Students also have the opportunity to work with health visitors, community midwives and increasingly with nurse practitioners and practice nurses.

The challenge in adult nursing is to get to know patients as individuals and to provide care and support that meets the individual's hopes and aspirations. The rewards are being able to help people recover fully or to remain well despite having a chronic disease.

Case history

Catherine Baker is studying nursing on the adult branch. She is a third year degree student and attends the Nightingale Institute, part of King's College London.

I've wanted to be a nurse since my early teens. I did three A levels and joined the degree programme straight from school. I enjoyed the programme. I enjoyed the variety. I was able to work in many different areas. My mentors were very supportive. On this course we are able to choose one area to specialise in. I chose care of older people because it's so interesting.

This is my last placement and I will qualify soon. I am going to work on a rotational staff development programme at St Thomas' Hospital in London. The programme is 18 months long and we have two placements, one on the medical unit for 9 months and one on the surgical unit. During the programme we have seven study days and also take a course in venepuncture and a mentorship course. Those of us who complete the course successfully are ready for a senior staff nurse post at the end.

My top priority on qualifying is to improve my clinical skills.

CHILDREN'S NURSING

Children's nurses care for newborns and people up to the age of 18. Children's nursing is very different from adult nursing.

THE ROLE OF THE CHILDREN'S NURSE

- Care for newborn babies.
- Care for children of all ages.
- Support the child's family and help them to care for their child.
- Work with the child and the family to plan care.
- Work as part of a professional team.
- Care for sick children.

Children react to illness in different ways and need specialist nurses who understand how illness affects children. Specially trained children's nurses understand how illness and injury affect children physically and psychologically and can offer them specialist support and care.

Children, like adults, are cared for in hospitals and in community settings. Advances in health care have led to children being discharged home from hospital more quickly than in the past. In hospital, sick children are normally cared for on special children's wards. The atmosphere here is very different from that on an adult ward. The aim is to put children at ease and to minimise the anxiety caused by a hospital stay. Parents are encouraged to stay with their child during hospital admissions. The children's nurse often works closely with parents. Sometimes parents are unable to stay with the sick child because they have other children or live some distance away. Then the nurse has to do his or her best to comfort the child and be a temporary substitute parent.

In hospitals children's nurses gain experience in neonatal intensive care units, maternity units, children's wards, theatre, children's outpatients departments and accident and emergency. In community settings children's nurses gain experience working with midwives, school nurses and health visitors. They may also work with specialist teams such as children's palliative care teams.

The child's world centres on home and family and a child's illness usually affects a whole family. Parents, brothers and sisters and other family members can be very upset by a child's illness. The children's nurse needs to develop skills to enable parents and other family members to express fears and he or she must have the ability to offer support in difficult times. Children's nurses also support, advise and educate parents and other close relatives. Once qualified, it is possible for children's nurses to specialise in hospital and community settings in areas such as burns and plastic surgery, intensive care, child protection and palliative care.

Communication skills are important in all aspects of nursing but they are especially important for children's nurses. The children's nurse must learn to communicate with young children, to work with doctors and other members of the team and to communicate effectively with worried parents who may be too upset to absorb information well. The children's nurse must also have a sense of fun and have the ability to enter into a child's world and to provide comfort, cuddles and care.

The challenges of children's nursing include working with very sick children, especially in palliative care. The rewards are in supporting families to care for children and in seeing children recover from illness and accident.

LEARNING DISABILITY NURSING

Learning disability nursing is the smallest branch of nursing. There are fewer than 10,000 learning disability nurses in the UK. The term 'learning disability' refers to people with a wide range of abilities and has been defined by the Department of Health as:

- reduced ability to understand new or complex information, to learn new skills (impaired intelligence);

- reduced ability to cope independently (impaired social functioning);

- a condition, which started before adulthood, with a lasting effect on development.

Learning disability may be a consequence of brain damage or malformation, which may have arisen before birth, childhood or adolescence. A learning disability cannot be cured, but education, health and social care can help minimise the effect of the disability and help people with a learning disability to achieve their potential.

THE ROLE OF THE LEARNING DISABILITY NURSE

- Identify factors that affect the health and well-being of the individual.

- Work with the person to help that individual to develop the ability to maintain and improve health.

- Work as part of a team to help the individual to develop new skills and abilities.

- Teach others about learning disability.

- Support families when a family member has learning disability.

- Provide care during crisis or when a person is unable to meet care needs independently.

People with a learning disability can find it difficult to manage and plan some aspects of everyday life. In the past the public and nursing profession did not always recognise the potential of people with learning disabilities and many people with learning disabilities were cared for in large hospitals. Now the role of nurses caring for people with learning disabilities has changed and registered nurses and health care assistants work with people with learning disabilities to help them reach their fullest potential.

Some people with mild learning disability may only require support and help from nurses at times of crisis or at particular points in their lives, for example a young person with mild learning disability may require help and support in finding a job. Some people who have learning disability may also have physical disabilities. In such cases the nurse will work with other professionals such as physiotherapists, occupational therapists and doctors to provide care and promote independence. In some cases the person with learning disability may need intensive support because of physical conditions or severe learning disabilities.

Learning disability nurses work in a variety of settings. The nurse may work in the community helping and supporting families when a child within the family has learning disability. He or she may use specialist skills to support the family in helping the person with learning disability to learn the skills required to be as independent as possible. The nurse may work in a house where a group of people with learning disabilities live; or in a care home where people who have severe learning disabilities live. There are also opportunities for learning disability nurses to work in schools. As learning disability nurses progress in their careers they can choose to continue to work with people in all setting or to specialise in an area such as sensory disability, education, or management of learning disability services.

The nurse may work with a team of specialists including doctors and psychologists to assess the degree of learning disability and the degree of help required. The nurse then develops what is known in general nursing as a care plan but, in learning disability nursing, is often known as a life plan.

The emphasis is not to provide care but to help prepare the person to live a full life.

The learning disability nurse's role is to help all people who have learning disability to lead a full life and to participate fully in society as equal members. This might mean helping the person develop the skills required to shop and buy food and to cook a meal using that food. It might mean helping a child with learning disability to learn to wash, dress and use the toilet independently.

As a learning disability nurse, the challenge is to remain constantly sensitive and alert to how you relate to people. People who have learning disability take time to make progress but small changes can make a huge difference to a person's quality of life. At times you may have to speak out strongly in the interests of the person with learning disability and challenge prejudices. You also need to develop the skills to support people and help them to speak up for themselves. This helps increase these people's self-confidence and ability to take part fully in life.

MENTAL HEALTH NURSING

Mental health nursing is the second largest branch of nursing. Some nurses choose the mental health branch while others gain mental health qualifications after becoming an adult nurse. The mental health nurse's role is varied.

THE ROLE OF THE MENTAL HEALTH NURSE

- Support people with enduring mental health needs in the community.

- Provide acute interventions in inpatient settings.

- Work with the person to assess needs and develop a plan of care.

- Administer medication and monitor its effects.

- Work with the person to help improve understanding of the condition.
- Help people with mental health needs to remain well.
- Work with groups of people with specific needs.
- Work as part of a team.

Mental health nursing has changed a great deal in recent years. In the past many people with mental health needs were cared for in large psychiatric hospitals. Now there is a greater emphasis in caring for people in the community. Advances in drug therapy mean that many people who required daily medication can be given long-acting medicines and their care can now be supervised in the community by community psychiatric nurses (see Chapter 7 for further details).

In hospitals people with mental health needs were once cared for on general wards. The general ward might have people with a range of needs, for example people with personality disorders such as schizophrenia, and problems with substance abuse. Now wards are increasingly specialised. The person with substance abuse problems is often cared for on a ward where all the patients have similar problems. People cared for in wards are now more acutely ill than in the past.

People are now living longer and older people are more likely to develop Alzheimer's disease and other types of dementia. Mental health nurses in acute wards care for people who have behavioural problems. People with dementia are also supported at home, in sheltered accommodation, in care homes and in specialist homes for people with dementia.

The challenges of mental nursing are retaining humanity and sensitivity when working in pressurised environments with acutely ill people. The rewards are in enabling people who reach crisis to recover and resume a normal life.

Case history

Remi Yussuf is 24 and in her first year of the mental health branch of a diploma programme at Kingston University, Surrey.

I've always wanted to help people and began doing voluntary work in a nursing home in Essex when I was 16. I really enjoyed it there and they offered me a part-time post when I was still studying. I left school at 16 and went to sixth form college. I did a GNVQ, an advanced GNVQ and a higher national diploma in performing arts. Then I went to work as a support worker with Luton and Dunstable NHS Trust caring for people with learning disabilities.

I decided that I'd like to become a registered nurse and applied to Kingston University because my family lived nearby. I'm really enjoying the course and my placements. I chose mental health nursing because I wanted to have the ability to get to know the person behind the mental illness and to be able to make a difference to the person's recovery.

Nursing is a varied profession. You can choose as a nurse to care for children, adults, people with learning disabilities or people with mental health needs. Each branch of nursing offers the opportunity to work in hospital or in the community and to specialise in a particular aspect of care.

2

Entry routes and application

This chapter aims to give you information about qualifications required for nursing education programmes. If you do not have the required qualifications you will find information here about how to obtain relevant qualifications. This chapter also provides information on diploma and degree courses and bursaries and grants. There is also information on how to apply for a place. Chapter 10 includes contact details of most of the organisations referred to in this chapter.

ENTRY QUALIFICATIONS

People who wish to apply to study nursing must have certain entry qualifications. The minimum qualifications required in England, Scotland and Northern Ireland are:

- Five GCSE passes at grade C or above. These must normally be obtained in one sitting. Some subjects, such as needlework or home economics, are not accepted.

- NVQ level 3 in a relevant subject, such as care.

- GNVQ advanced level qualifications in a relevant subject.

There are a number of equivalent qualifications and you can check these on the Nursing and Midwifery Council (NMC) Web site. At present the minimum entry qualifications are being reviewed and they may change in 2004. It is advisable to check with the NMC before applying to study nursing. The minimum qualifications required are set by law. Some universities may require additional qualifications. For example, some universities stipulate that nursing students have a qualification in English, a science subject and mathematics. Students who wish to study on the degree programme are normally required to have *at least* two GCSE A level passes.

In Wales students are required to have A level qualifications or equivalent. You can obtain further details from Health Professionals Wales or from the Universities and Colleges Admissions Service (UCAS). Applicants who obtained their qualifications more than five years ago may be required to demonstrate evidence of recent study.

Cadet nursing

Cadet schemes were once very popular with young people who wished to become nurses. They were discontinued some years ago but are now being reintroduced all over the UK. Modern cadet schemes are aimed not just at young people who wish to become nurses but also those who wish to work in other areas of health care. They are designed to help people aged 16–19 obtain the qualifications needed to begin professional study. Nursing cadets can either choose to enter a general cadet scheme that starts by giving them some experience of working in different areas such as physiotherapy, occupational therapy, pharmacy and nursing or choose to enter a scheme specific to nursing.

Entry criteria

The entry requirements for cadet schemes vary from one NHS Trust to another. Some Trusts will not require formal qualifications but all will look for evidence of skills such as the ability to listen and to communicate effectively.

Some NHS Trusts have an arrangement with their local university so that successful cadets are guaranteed an interview on nurse education programmes. Some Trusts also have arrangements that guarantee successful cadets preferential status when applying for nurse education programmes.

Types of cadet scheme

There is no one recognised national or UK-wide cadet scheme. Each scheme has been designed by an individual NHS Trust so the schemes vary. They usually consist of a one- to two-year programme that enables cadets to work under the supervision of experienced staff and also take part in a training programme. Cadets who wish to enter one of the other professions such as radiography, dietetics or speech and language therapy can follow a course leading to them obtaining recognised entry qualifications for that particular profession. Nurse cadet training programmes lead to a recognised qualification such as an Access to nursing award or an NVQ level 3 award in care. Other cadet schemes are designed to follow the BTEC in Health Studies higher diploma route, and successful completion meets the minimum entry requirements for nursing and some other health care professions' education programmes.

Finding out more about cadet schemes

There are two main ways in which you can find out more about cadet schemes. You can contact the HR department of your local NHS Trust. The staff there will provide up-to-date information about local schemes within the Trust.

You can also contact your local Workforce Development Confederation. Workforce Development Confederations (formerly known as Education and Training Consortia) bring together groups of NHS Trusts, universities and colleges to coordinate health care training provision within each local area. NHS Careers can also provide brief information about some of the cadet schemes in England.

NVQ entry

If you are not working and have been unemployed for six months or more you may be eligible for free NVQ training. You can find out about this scheme from your local college of further education. If you are working as a health care assistant in a hospital, a care home or in the community you can apply to do an NVQ course. Many employers are willing to support you and give you time off to study. It is important to sign up for an NVQ level 3 course as NVQ level 2 courses do not meet nursing entry requirements.

Most NVQ courses consist of theory and practical work that aim to develop skills and knowledge. Courses vary but many NVQ level 3 courses consist of one day's study per week for around 20–26 weeks. This study, known as the knowledge component of the NVQ, may be delivered in your workplace or in a college of further education. NVQ students are required to keep a portfolio of evidence to show that they have met NVQ standards. NVQ students are assessed by a specially trained assessor who checks that each competency has been met. The assessor may be a colleague in your workplace or an assessor from the college may come to assess you.

Access to nursing

Access courses are for adults without formal qualifications. Successful completion of an access course is considered to be the equivalent of two A levels and enables students to enter higher education. Access courses are available on a full- and part-time basis.

People applying for nursing or midwifery courses must successfully complete a *full* access course. Some colleges offer a shortened access course for people who have some academic qualifications. This is not acceptable for nursing and midwifery education. The access course should consist of at least four subjects including anatomy and physiology and study skills.

Only access courses accredited by the Quality Assurance Agency (QAA) for Higher Education are acceptable for nursing and midwifery education. Some small privately run colleges claim to run access courses but if these are not accredited they are of no value to people who wish to study nursing or midwifery. See Chapter 10 for details of where to find further information.

Students with degrees

Students with a degree in a subject other than nursing or midwifery can apply for an accelerated programme at either diploma or degree level. Degree qualified applicants often complete a diploma or degree programme in two years. The careers advisory board in the country you wish to study can advise you on this (see Chapter 10 for details).

TYPES OF TRAINING DIPLOMA OR DEGREE

In the past nurses were educated on the wards and in schools of nursing attached to local hospitals. There were then two levels of nurses, those who studied for two years were known as state enrolled nurses. Those who studied for three years were known as state registered nurses. Few nurses studied to degree level. Nurse education moved to the university sector some years ago. Enrolled nurse education programmes were discontinued. The minimum qualification for registered nurses moved to diploma level and degree programmes became more widespread. Degree programmes were often four years long while diploma programmes lasted three years.

At the time of writing the nursing profession is again debating whether all registered nurses should in the future be qualified to degree level. In Wales the decision has already been made and all nursing students there now qualify with a degree. Nursing degree programmes and Honours degree programmes are now normally three years long, the same length as a diploma programme. In England, Scotland and Northern Ireland many people choose to enter the diploma programme rather than the degree programme because diploma bursaries are more generous than student grants. In Wales, where degree students qualify for more generous bursaries, competition for places is growing each year.

Degree programmes are more academically demanding and entry criteria are more stringent so some applicants who would be successful in obtaining a place to study a diploma in nursing may be unsuccessful in obtaining a place on a degree programme. Increasingly, nurses who wish to gain promotion at ward manager level or beyond are required to have degree level qualifications. Diploma students can top up their diploma to a degree after registration by studying full- or part-time after registration.

FUNDING

Secondments

Health care assistants who work in the NHS may be eligible to apply for a secondment. Seconded students receive their normal HCA salary, which is considerably more than a student bursary, throughout their education programme. In order to be eligible for a secondment the applicant must have worked for the NHS Trust for a minimum of one year and meet entry requirements. Secondment places are limited – most NHS Trusts only have one or two places a year – so competition is keen. If you are a health care worker interested in this route into nursing education, your manager or the HR department in your NHS Trust can provide details.

Bursaries

An NHS bursary is a grant awarded to eligible students to cover everyday living costs such as food and accommodation while they are completing their education. Overseas applicants must have been resident in the UK for three years prior to the start of the course in order to qualify for a bursary. The NHS bursary is a non-means-tested grant. In England, Scotland and Northern Ireland, students studying on the diploma programmes are eligible for bursaries. In Wales diploma programmes are no longer available, those who wish to become nurses or midwives must complete a three-year Honours degree programme. Degree students in Wales are eligible for bursaries.

Table 2.1 Bursaries levels 2004

Age under 26 at start of programme		Age over 26 at start of programme
In London	£6,250	£6,850
Outside London	£5,560	£6,216

Further allowances may also be payable:

- for initial expenses;
- for dependents;
- to single parents;
- to disabled students;
- for having two homes;
- for clinical placement costs;
- to students entering training from Social Services Care.

The NHS also pays university tuition fees on behalf of students. Bursaries are not subject to income tax, national insurance or pension deductions. The bursary is paid in 12 equal monthly amounts. The first instalment of the bursary is paid by cheque and then it is paid into the student's bank account.

Grants

Degree students who are studying in England, Scotland and Northern Ireland can apply for an NHS means-tested bursary (this is normally known as a grant). The amount awarded via this means-tested grant is decided taking into account your income, the income of your parents if you are under 25 unless you have been supporting yourself for three years and your spouse's income if you are married.

Grant regulations are complex and change every year. Chapter 10 provides details of where to find further information.

FURTHER FINANCIAL HELP

Income support

Full-time students are not normally entitled to income support and housing benefits. Exceptions are:

- single parents with a dependent child under 16;
- disabled students;

▓ one of a couple with dependent children under 16 where the partner is not in full-time study;

▓ couples who are both students and have dependants under 16 – these can claim income support and housing benefit during the summer vacation but not at any other time.

Council tax

The rules relating to council tax are complex. In principle full-time students are exempt from council tax. In practice this depends on where you live and who you live with.

▓ Students who live in halls of residence are exempt.

▓ Students who live with other students are not liable.

▓ Students who live with non-students are usually liable to pay council tax.

Your chosen university can give you further advice.

Childcare costs

NHS-funded students will be eligible for means-tested allowances to cover up to 85 per cent of the costs of childcare from September 2004. The allowances are available for children up to the age of 15 (or age 17 if a child has special needs). The allowances are up to £114 a week for students with one eligible child and up to £170 a week for two or more eligible children. These allowances will be available to eligible students, new and existing. Chapter 10 gives details of how to find out if you are eligible.

ACCOMMODATION

Students are normally expected to find their own accommodation. Sometimes accommodation is available on a short-term basis for students in university halls of residence or in hospital accommodation. Universities and hospitals often keep lists of flats and houses, which are often shared by a number of students to keep costs down. Staff noticeboards and intranet sites in universities and hospitals may offer a large selection of accommodation. There can be a scramble for accommodation just before the start of a course so it is important to look around and act quickly if you find something suitable.

Students who have left home for the first time often feel lost and homesick at first. If you are feeling like this, you will probably find that this stage passes. You will adjust to your new life and make friends who you may keep in touch with throughout your life.

Mature students usually choose to study locally because of family ties. They also face a major period of readjustment, however research shows that mature students with families settle into nursing and cope well academically, often outshining their younger colleagues.

APPLYING FOR A PLACE

The process of applying for a place differs in each of the four countries within the UK.

England

You can obtain information from NHS Careers (see Chapter 10).

Nursing and Midwifery Diploma programmes

UCAS manages a clearing house called the Nursing and Midwifery Admissions Service (NMAS). NMAS processes all applications for full-time and accelerated nursing and midwifery diplomas.

You can obtain an application package online or by telephoning or writing to NMAS. This guide is also available in reference libraries. The application pack contains a guide to the educational requirements in the country you wish to train in, details of courses offered and universities offering these. The guide contains an application form. If you decide to apply you must complete the form and pay the appropriate fee. You can make up to four choices for a fee of £10. If you make a single choice the fee is £5.

If you wish to be accepted in the autumn it is wise to apply a year in advance. NMAS has a fixed application period. Each year prospective students can apply from September to the 15 December to obtain places in the autumn of the following year and the spring of the year after that.

Applications received between 16 December and 30 June are treated as late applications. NMAS will not consider any applications received after 30 June and recommend that applicants contact the university directly. All applications that have been received before the closing date are considered first. Only when these have been considered are late applications forwarded to the universities selected by the applicant.

Degree programmes in nursing and midwifery

UCAS manage applications for nursing and midwifery degree programmes. Applications should be submitted in the autumn of the year before the course starts. UCAS has a fixed application period from 1 September to 15 January. Applications received after15 January but before 30 June will be considered late applications. Any applications received after 30 June will be subject to clearing.

Northern Ireland

In Northern Ireland diploma and degree programmes are offered, you must contact the universities directly.

Queen's University Belfast offers both diploma and degree programmes. Applicants apply directly to Queen's University Belfast. Those who are accepted are assessed at the end of the first year and the most academically able are offered the opportunity to complete their studies at degree level.

The University of Ulster offers degree and Honours degree courses that last for three years. The Honours degree programme is very popular and entry criteria are stringent. Competition for places is keen. The university also offers a degree programme which is very popular, but students who are unable to obtain a place on the Honours programme may be more successful in obtaining a place on the degree programme. You can obtain further information from the University of Ulster and details about entry criteria are available on the Web site. Admission is through UCAS.

Wales

Careers information can be obtained from Health Professional Wales. In Wales all nursing and midwifery educational programmes are now at Honours degree level. The nursing student completes a three-year programme and is awarded a Bachelor of Nursing Honours degree and is able to register as a nurse. In Wales degree students are offered the same level of financial support as diploma students in the rest of the UK. Competition for places is keen and there are four applicants for every student place in Wales. Applicants who are unsuccessful are advised what further qualifications or experience they require to improve their chances of obtaining a place.

Applications are via UCAS and should begin 12–18 months before you aim to commence your nurse education programme. If you wish to commence studying between Autumn 2005 and Spring 2006 you must apply between September 2004 and 15 January 2005. It may be possible in August 2005 to make a late application but as demand for places in Wales is so high this option is much less reliable than in the other UK countries. If you do not apply early for a place in Wales you may well be disappointed.

Scotland

Nursing and midwifery diploma programmes
In Scotland the Central Applications for Nursing and Midwifery (CATCH) processes applications for full length and accelerated nursing diplomas and midwifery diplomas. You can obtain information about available programmes and entry requirements from Careers Information Scotland.

Degree programmes in nursing and midwifery
Applicants for degree programmes apply through UCAS.

Part-time courses

Some universities run part-time courses, these are often run in term time and have shorter days than full-time courses. They aim to enable people with caring responsibilities to study. Some universities have approval to run such courses but do not offer them at present. If you wish to find out about part-time courses contact the careers advisory service in the country where you wish to study or contact directly the university at which you wish to study.

Age limits

In England, Scotland and Northern Ireland you can begin nurse education from the age of 17. In Wales you must be 18 or over to begin a degree programme. There is no upper age limit and the life experience of older students is valued.

The application process

There are four parts to the application process: short-listing, interview, occupational health screening and police checks.

Short-listing

Applicants apply for a place at a university and that university checks that the person has appropriate qualifications. Most universities will offer candidates with the appropriate qualifications an interview. When competition for places is intense, as it is in Wales and on many degree programmes, universities may short-list candidates. This means that candidates who have the minimum qualifications may not be offered an interview if there are better qualified candidates applying.

Interview

Candidates who are short-listed will be invited to interview. Interviews vary from university to university but all universities will have an interview with the opportunity for you to ask questions. Some interviews also have a written test to check your communication, literacy and numeracy skills. Some interviews also have a group discussion where a group of applicants discuss a particular issue. This aims to check that you are not so quiet that you do not participate or so dominant that you prevent others from participating.

Health screening

Candidates who are successful at interview are screened by the occupational health department to ensure that they are fit enough to cope with the demands of nursing.

Police checks

People working with vulnerable people in health care (and other settings) must have an enhanced police disclosure. This means that the Criminal Records Bureau checks the person's police record. An enhanced disclosure reveals not only actual convictions but also cautions and cases where a person was interviewed in relation to a crime but not actually convicted or charged. Driving convictions such as speeding where a person has more than three penalty points on his or her licence are counted as a criminal record.

Normally if some years have elapsed since a conviction the conviction is 'wiped' from police records under a law known as the Rehabilitation of Offenders Act. These convictions show up under enhanced disclosures.

Applicants should disclose all convictions, cautions and details of interviews with the police in relation to crime. These do not necessarily prevent you being accepted on a place as each case is judged individually.

The widest possible choice

Nursing is changing at a rapid pace and is becoming more attractive to people from all walks of life. In some countries, such as Wales and Northern Ireland there is intense competition for places. In some parts of the UK, such as London, where the cost of living is high there is less competition for certain places on certain courses. If you are studying for qualifications at present get the best grades that you can so that you have the widest possible choice of where to study and what course to study on.

TOP TIPS

- Make copies of your application form and complete a copy. Transfer the information in the copy neatly onto the form. Copy the completed form and keep it for reference.

- Put your qualifications in a folder. You will be asked to show these and they will be copied.

- Ensure that you meet the minimum requirements of the course.

- Find out as much as you can about nursing before making your application.

- Be clear that you can meet the demands of the course and are fully committed to studying for a nursing qualification.

- Decide which branch of nursing you would like to study.

- Be prepared to answer questions about why you have chosen this branch.

- Arrive early for your interview.

- Dress neatly.

- Ask questions during the application process and during the interview.

3

Midwifery

Midwifery is quite different from nursing although it shares some common characteristics. Midwives have long been professionals in their own right whereas nurses have had to battle to be accepted as professionals.

Nursing, despite recent innovations in health promotion, is a therapeutic and curative profession. Most people who are cared for by nurses expect a cure or improvement in disease. Midwives, though, normally look after healthy women who are pregnant. People who are cared for by midwives expect a healthy baby. Midwives have been caring for women as people, not as patients, for many years, as 90 per cent of pregnant women are in good health.

Midwives do encounter some difficulties in practising as true professionals in hospital settings if medical staff view pregnancy as a disease and see pregnant women as 'sick' rather than healthy women undergoing normal changes brought on by pregnancy. Some midwives prefer to practise independently or in community settings where these difficulties are rarer.

THE MIDWIFE'S ROLE

The term midwife means 'with woman' and the aim of midwifery is to be with the woman and help and support her through pregnancy, delivery and early parenthood. The midwife becomes involved in the care of the pregnant woman as soon as pregnancy is confirmed. The continuity of care that midwives offer has been proven to reduce the risk of complications and lead to higher levels of normal births.

Midwives offer pregnant women support and health education. They run parent craft classes, which help mothers and fathers to learn about baby care before the baby arrives. Midwives run antenatal classes and explain the normal changes of pregnancy and also run their own clinics. They obtain detailed information, known as a history, about the pregnant woman's general health and monitor her health and well-being throughout the pregnancy. The midwife is fully competent to care for most women throughout pregnancy. If the midwife detects actual or potential problems with the pregnancy or the delivery then he or she is legally required to call in a doctor.

Most women choose to use NHS services for care before, during and after delivery. Women using NHS services have a choice about the type of care given before the birth, where the baby is born and the type of care given after the birth. They can choose to have midwife-only care; care that is delivered by the GP and the midwife; care that is delivered by the hospital and the GP, or hospital care overseen by a consultant:

■ Midwife-only care. Pregnant women can choose to have all of their care delivered by a midwife. This type of care is usually delivered by a team of midwives and every effort will be made to ensure that the pregnant women is normally seen by the same midwife throughout the pregnancy. This type of care gives mothers the opportunity to know the midwife or midwives who will assist at the birth.

■ Midwife and GP care. The midwife and the GP share the pregnant woman's care. Antenatal care is shared between the midwife and the GP and is delivered at antenatal clinics at the GP surgery. Either the midwife or the GP can run these clinics.

■ Hospital and GP care. Hospital consultants and the GP share the pregnant woman's care and antenatal clinics and help at the local hospital or birthing centre and at the GP surgery. Pregnant women who choose this option still attend parent craft classes run by midwives.

■ Hospital care. The pregnant woman receives care during pregnancy (and normally during delivery) from midwives and medical staff. A hospital consultant who specialises in the care of pregnant women will oversee the care.

Women are entirely free to choose the type of care they wish. However, the midwife has a duty to assess the pregnant woman and to recommend appropriate care. If the woman has a long-term problem that may affect her or the baby in pregnancy then the midwife will recommend the appropriate care. If the woman develops actual or potential complications the midwife will call in a doctor. Midwives are legally required to attend to a woman even if the woman declines to heed medical advice and accept medical attention.

The midwife is a specialist in normal maternity care; at over 75 per cent of births the midwife is the senior professional in attendance. The midwife is the only person, other than a doctor (who need not be specially trained), who is legally able to deliver babies.

Midwives also provide care and support to mother and baby for up to 28 days after delivery. This can be extended in special circumstances. After delivery the midwife checks that the mother is recovering normally from the birth and that the baby is developing normally. The midwife provides support and practical help and advice about baby care and feeding.

The midwife's role has been defined by the regulatory body for nursing and midwifery (formerly the UKCC) and that definition is set out below.

THE ROLE OF THE MIDWIFE

■ Provide sound family planning information and advice.

■ Diagnose pregnancies and monitor normal pregnancies; carry out examinations necessary for the monitoring of the development of normal pregnancies.

- Prescribe or advise on the examinations necessary for the earliest possible diagnosis of pregnancies at risk.

- Provide a programme of parenthood preparation and a complete preparation for childbirth including advice on hygiene and nutrition.

- Care for and assist the mother during labour and monitor the condition of the foetus by the appropriate clinical and technical means.

- Conduct spontaneous deliveries including, where required, an episiotomy and, in urgent cases, a breech delivery.

- Recognise the warning signs of abnormality in the mother or infant which necessitate referral to a doctor and assist the latter where appropriate; take the necessary emergency measures in the doctor's absence, in particular the manual removal of the placenta, possibly followed by a manual examination of the uterus.

- Examine and care for the newborn infant; taking all initiatives which are necessary in case of need and carrying out, where necessary, immediate resuscitation.

Is midwifery the career for you?

The Royal College of Midwives have defined what qualities professionals and the public expect of midwives. A midwife should be:

- intuitive, kind, caring and objective;

- able to act as an advocate for women and take responsibility for his or her own actions;

- a good team player, able to work in partnership with other professionals;

- flexible and adaptable to mothers' circumstances and needs;

▓ prepared to look after all women, irrespective of class, creed, economic status, race or age;

▓ able to accept women and the circumstances in which they live;

▓ professional and maintain accurate and contemporaneous records.

MIDWIFERY EDUCATION

There are two main ways to become a registered midwife. You can complete a pre-registration midwifery programme or gain a post-registration qualification in midwifery after qualifying as a nurse.

Pre-registration programmes

Pre-registration programmes, often known as the direct entry programme, allow people who are not nurses to become midwives. These are available at degree and diploma level in all UK countries other than Wales, which only offers degree-level programmes. Pre-registration programmes have the same minimum entry qualifications as nursing diploma and degree programmes. There are around 2,000 places on midwifery programmes in the UK each year so there are far fewer available places than on nursing programmes. Midwifery is a popular career choice especially for women who have been cared for by midwives when they had their own children. Many mothers dream of becoming midwives and helping other mothers.

Direct entry programmes are particularly appealing to mature women with children and competition for places can be keen. Midwifery is intensely rewarding but is also hard work and some universities prefer applicants who have some experience of working in midwifery settings. Some candidates choose to work in hospital maternity units or GP surgeries so they can get an idea of what the role involves. If you do not have entry qualifications, working as a care assistant can give you the opportunity to find out about the role and also to gain NVQ level 3 entry qualifications.

In the past, people who wanted to become midwives were required to become registered nurses and then to qualify as a midwife. Pre-registration programmes make becoming a midwife more direct but there may be disadvantages to this route. Some senior posts require people who are registered nurses and registered midwives. Registered midwives can become registered nurses if they study on a shortened nurse education programme. This is usually two years long.

Post-registration education

Registered nurses (adult branch) can complete an 18-month long post-registration education programme in midwifery. These are available in all four countries of the UK.

The application process

The careers advisory board in the country where you choose to practise can provide information about pre- and post-registration training programmes (contact information is in Chapter 10). The application process differs in each UK country. Chapter 2 gives details of how to apply for pre-registration programmes in each of the UK countries.

The careers advisory board in the country where you choose to work can also provide details of post-registration education in midwifery. You can also search for details of all courses on the Internet (look under Course search in Chapter 10 for the link).

WORKING AS A REGISTERED MIDWIFE

Newly registered midwives often choose to work in a hospital where it is possible to gain experience in a number of different areas. The midwife may choose to work on the labour ward or in a birthing centre for low-risk mothers, in antenatal care or in a special care baby unit. The midwife who has gained experience can choose to develop his or her career in many different ways.

Community midwife

Midwifery education is composed of 50 per cent theory and 50 per cent practice. Midwives work in the community for long periods during their education programmes and many choose to work as community midwives after registration. A midwife must have two years' post-registration experience before applying for a post as a community midwife.

Professional updating

To practise as a midwife, you must be registered with the statutory body for nursing, midwifery and health visiting. This is the Nursing and Midwifery Council. Practising midwives are legally required to notify the NMC on an annual basis of their intention to practise. To remain on the register, you must update your knowledge and maintain a professional portfolio as evidence of your updating.

Returning to practice

Many midwives qualify, work for some years and leave between the ages of 29 and 35, perhaps to bring up a family. Midwives who have not worked as midwives for a minimum of 12 weeks in the last five years or who have not notified the Nursing and Midwifery Council of their intention to practise must complete a return to practice course. Many return to practice courses are run on a part-time basis and have 'family friendly' hours to enable midwives with children to attend while children are at school.

Midwives who have returned from working abroad may have gained a wealth of clinical experience and enhanced their practice in many ways. However, because of the way that midwifery is organised in other countries, they may need to update certain aspects of their practice such as antenatal or postnatal care.

The NHS meets all fees for midwives returning to practice in the NHS. Financial support is available but this varies between different NHS Trusts. You can obtain details of support from your local NHS Trust or the NHS Workforce Development Confederation (see Chapter 10 for contact details). Your local NHS workforce development team will have a special return to practice coordinator, who can advise you on all aspects of returning to midwifery.

All refresher courses are individually tailored to the midwife and the length of the course is dependent on the length of time the midwife has not been practising. The content of the course will also vary.

Many midwives who completed their return to practice course apply for full-, part-time or bank work with the NHS Trust where the course was carried out. The midwife may choose to work elsewhere if he or she wishes.

CAREER PATHWAYS

Registered midwives, like all newly qualified professionals, require time to gain skills before seeking promotion. The experienced midwife has a number of career options. He or she may wish to work as a community midwife or may wish to develop a career in clinical practice. Midwives have the opportunity to specialise in a number of areas, such as intensive care of newborn babies (neonatal intensive care), public health or parenting education. The midwife has the opportunity to become a clinical specialist or a consultant midwife. Many universities run Master's degree programmes that can help prepare for such roles.

The midwife may choose to teach or to combine clinical practice with teaching in a lecturer practitioner role. Midwives who choose to teach at university can gain a teaching qualification such as a degree in education (Bachelor of Education) if qualified at diploma level. Midwives with degrees can choose from postgraduate qualifications such as the postgraduate certificate, diploma or Master's degree in education.

Some midwives choose to be involved in clinical or academic research. Some midwives working in community and hospital settings choose a career in management. Universities run a range of degree and postgraduate management qualifications that help prepare midwives for management roles. Some midwives choose to work abroad on either a working holiday, long term or on a voluntary basis. Many midwives choose to work part-time because of family commitments. It is possible to develop your career and to work part-time within the NHS.

PAY AND CONDITIONS

NHS employees (other than senior managers and doctors) are now moving to a unified structure of pay and conditions known as Agenda for Change. Under Agenda for Change all employees will be placed within certain bands depending on the skills and knowledge required for the person to carry out a particular role. You will find details of Agenda for Change pay bands in Chapter 4.

Working conditions

All NHS staff will work 37.5 hours per week. This is the normal working week for midwives and nurses. NHS staff in pay bands 1–7, who work outside of 'normal working hours' of 7.00 am to 7.00 pm or on Saturdays, Sundays or Bank Holidays receive enhanced or 'unsocial hours' payments. Details of these payments are given in Table 3.1. Staff in pay band 8 receive unsocial hours payments on Bank Holidays, between 10.00 pm and 7.00 am weekdays and from 1.00 pm until 9.00 am at weekends.

Table 3.1 Unsocial hours payments

Average unsocial hours per week	Percentage basic pay Bands 1–7	Percentage basic pay Band 8
Up to 5	Local agreement	Local agreement
Between 5 and 9	9%	9%
Between 9 and 13	13%	10%
Between 13 and 17	17%	10%
Between 17 and 21	21%	10%
More than 21	25%	10%

Annual leave is calculated on length of NHS service. On appointment staff are entitled to 27 days + 8 days Bank Holidays. After five years' service staff are entitled to 29 days + 8 days Bank Holidays. After 10 years' service staff are entitled to 33 days + 8 days Bank Holidays.

On-call payments are paid to staff who may be called for advice or asked to come into work if required. Details of on-call enhancements are in Table 3.2.

Table 3.2   On-call payments

Frequency of on-call	Value of enhancement
1 day in 3 or more	9.5%
Between 1 in 3 and 1 in 6 days	4.5%
Between 1 in 9 and 1 in 6 days	3%
Between 1 in 12 and 1 in 9	2%
Less than 1 in 12	Local agreement

Staff who work in London and surrounding regions are paid an allowance to take account of the high cost of living there. There are three ranges of London allowance. These apply to inner London, outer London and the fringe of London. Staff within each of these areas is paid between the minimum and maximum London allowance. These are based on a percentage of salary. Table 3.3 gives details.

Table 3.3   London allowances

Area	Level
Inner London	20% of basic salary minimum £3,097 maximum £5,161
Outer London	15% of basic salary minimum £2,581 maximum £3,631
Fringe	5% of basic salary minimum £744 maximum £1,342

Midwifery is a unique career providing the opportunity to meet lots of new people and to support mothers before, during and after childbirth. The midwife has the option to remain in clinical practice, to work part- or full-time and to develop a satisfying career in clinical practice, teaching and management.

TOP TIPS

■ Find out as much as you can about midwifery before considering an application.

■ Make sure that midwifery is the career for you.

■ If possible, gain experience working as a volunteer or a health care assistant.

■ Use the Top tips in Chapter 2 to prepare for application and interview.

4

Working as a registered nurse

Working as a registered nurse is very different from being a student. The registered nurse's first job as a nurse is important. It enables nurses to learn how to put theory into practice and how to gain confidence in the skills acquired as a student. The newly registered nurse has to make the transition from being a student with few clinical responsibilities to the registered nurse dealing with a varied workload and competing pressures.

Consolidating your experience

Most student nurses in their final year of education begin to evaluate the wards where they are working as potential workplaces. Newly registered nurses normally apply for a post in the NHS Trust where they have gained experience in their final year of nurse education. Most newly registered nurses choose to gain their initial experience in a non-specialist area. The registered nurse who has followed the adult branch may choose to work on a general surgical or medical ward. The nurse may choose to work on another general ward after gaining six months' experience or may choose to work in a specialist area such as accident and emergency or intensive care.

The NMC recommends that each newly registered nurse must have a period of supervised practice. This period of supervised practice is known as preceptorship. This is normally a four-month period though some newly registered staff may require an extended period of support perhaps because they work part-time. In this period a more experienced registered nurse is appointed as a preceptor. The preceptor's role is to guide and assist the newly registered nurse in making the transition from student to registered and experienced practitioner. In some areas this support system is still not functioning effectively and newly registered nurses do not always get the support they require. Student nurses can check with newly registered colleagues about the level of support available in particular areas.

INDUCTION

When any employee goes to work in a new NHS Trust he or she is asked to attend an induction course. These courses are usually carried out in the hospital or community where the nurse will work. Induction courses for nurses are usually in two parts. The first few days of these courses are general induction days for all new staff working in the Trust. They cover general issues such as pay, conditions, sick leave policy and general health and safety. The next few days of an induction programme are often specific to a particular health care profession. Nurses often receive guidance on issues such as dispensing of medication, reporting of accidents and other nursing policies and procedures within the Trust. Most NHS Trusts also identify mandatory updating sessions, which nurses must attend at particular intervals. Typically nurses are required to attend mandatory annual updates on resuscitation and annual or biannual updates on moving and handling.

CAREER PATHWAYS

Some nurses who are unsure of which area they wish to work in may apply for a staff nurse development programme. Many NHS Trusts run these programmes. They usually consist of a rotation through different clinical areas such as medicine, surgery, accident and emergency. These programmes are 12–18 months long and are combined with a series of study days (and often support from an experienced mentor or dedicated lecturer practitioner) on clinical and managerial issues.

About six months after registration staff nurses remember their lack of confidence with astonishment and realise that they really began to learn about nursing after registration. This is the beginning of lifelong learning for the registered nurse.

At this point the staff nurse has learnt a great deal about nursing and even more about him- or herself. Usually the staff nurse moves on and gains another six months of general experience. If a staff nurse has worked in a surgical unit he or she may wish to gain experience in medicine or vice versa. Some nurses decide that they would like to work in the community, others that they would prefer to work in a particular speciality such as care of older people or minor injuries.

When a nurse has been registered for around a year he or she can begin to consider career options. Nurses can now choose to work in clinical practice, in education or in management. The journey and gaining the skills required can be an exciting experience.

A career in clinical practice

The registered nurse who wishes to specialise in a particular area of clinical practice obviously will need to gain specialist skills in that particular area. Universities now run courses or modules to enable nurses to gain particular knowledge and skills. Registered nurses are required to teach and assess student nurses and can gain these skills by taking a course in teaching and assessing in clinical practice. A recognised course in teaching and assessing is normally considered essential for nurses who wish to gain promotion. Newly registered nurses will be paid on pay band 5 of the Agenda for Change pay bands.

The nurse is usually required to undertake relevant courses to gain expertise in the area in which he or she has chosen to work. A nurse who chooses to work with older people, for example, might find courses in continence care, palliative care, care of older people and rehabilitation relevant. These courses are usually held at universities though some NHS Trusts run in-house courses. University-based courses and some in-house courses are run at three levels. Nurses can obtain a certificate of attendance. Nurses can practise the skills gained at a course under the supervision of an experienced nurse to gain a certificate of competency. Nurses may have the option of completing additional work, usually a project or pieces of written work, to gain academic credit.

A nurse educated under a traditional programme who does not have a diploma in nursing can use these credits to gain a diploma in nursing. A nurse who has a diploma in nursing may wish to build credits to use towards a degree. In order to gain a diploma a nurse must obtain 120 academic credits at level 2. Students require 120 level 2 credits and 120 level 3 credits to obtain a degree. Students can gain 90 credits from taught courses and gain the additional 30 credits required for a degree or diploma by completing an integrating study. It is possible to gain some academic credit for learning that has been formally assessed, this is known as APEL (accreditation of prior experiential learning). The university where you choose to study can advise you of their policy. Taught courses usually have 15 credits though some longer courses have 30 credits.

Nurses who have six months or more of relevant experience may be successful in gaining a post as a senior staff nurse. Evidence of relevant studies may give you the edge at short-listing and interview.

When the nurse has gained solid experience as a senior staff nurse he or she may wish to apply for a junior sister or charge nurse post. In hospital settings the junior sister's role is to support the senior sister in managing the ward and ensuring that patients receive high quality care. When applying for such posts it is important that you can demonstrate not only academic qualifications but also a range of experience and growing clinical and managerial skills. You can gain these skills as a staff nurse through mentoring and supporting students and undertaking projects to improve care.

The next rung in the ladder is the post of senior sister or ward manager, as it is known in some areas. The ward manager has 24-hour responsibility for care and staffing of his or her ward.

Growing numbers of employers are seeking evidence that you have or are working towards a degree. It looks likely that ward managers will be paid on band 6 or 7 of the Agenda for Change pay bands.

There are also opportunities for you to develop advanced roles as you move through your career.

Options beyond ward manager level

It is important that nurses who wish to develop as nurse specialists, teachers or managers gain solid nursing experience. Nurses who have gained a degree and experience at senior sister or ward manager level have a number of options.

Clinical nurse specialist

At present the law does not protect the title 'nurse specialist' and there are no mandatory qualifications for the role. In practice nurses who are called nurse specialists are working at many different levels. Some are working at the same level as a junior sister or a senior sister and others are practising at an advanced level. Some nurse specialists are required to have a degree and possibly to be working towards a Master's degree. Some are not required to have degree or even diploma level qualifications. Most nurse specialists are required to have significant expertise and be highly skilled in their speciality. Some specialists, including those who work with more senior specialists and nurse consultants, are still in the process of gaining expertise and qualifications. Under the old pay system nurse specialists were paid on different grades according to qualifications and expertise and the demands of the post. As Agenda for Change is introduced specialist posts will be assessed individually and the nurse will be placed on the appropriate pay band.

The NMC are currently launching a consultation to determine what skills and knowledge are required from nurses practising at advanced level.

Lecturer practitioner

The lecturer practitioner post enables nurses to develop both practice and teaching skills. Lecturer practitioners usually work as an expert practitioner within a particular speciality and also teach pre- and post-registration students in university. Many lecturer practitioners have what is known as a 'joint appointment' and are employed jointly by a university and an NHS Trust. Under Agenda for Change such posts will probably have to be graded on an individual level. A first degree is normally required and many lecturer practitioners are studying for MSc qualifications. Lecturer practitioners may aim to become nurse consultants or nurse teachers.

Nurse consultants

The nurse consultant's role was introduced in 2000 and is the most senior role within clinical practice. The nurse consultant's role consists of 50 per cent working with patients, 25 per cent education and 25 per cent strategy. The vast majority of nurse consultants have over 20 years' experience in their speciality and have a Master's degree. Some are continuing their studies to doctoral level. Nurse consultants will be paid on band 8 of the Agenda for Change pay bands. There are four categories in band 8: bands 8a, b, c and d. Each post will be evaluated to determine its band 8 grading.

A career in education

Only 1,000 registered nurses work in the education sector. The nurse who wishes to develop a career in nurse education normally starts off as a nurse lecturer and can progress to senior lecturer, principal lecturer and to head of the faculty of nurse education – this post is known as Dean.

The role of a nurse lecturer is varied and will include teaching, supporting students in clinical practice and planning lectures. The minimum qualification for a lecturer's post is a degree in nursing, five years' post-registration experience and experience of teaching and mentoring students in clinical practice. Many universities prefer lecturers to have a teaching qualification, to have published in a nursing journal and to have MSc level qualifications. Universities can find it difficult to attract suitable candidates and many are willing to support newly appointed lecturers and help them to obtain teaching qualifications such as the postgraduate certificate or diploma in education. Nurse lecturers work for universities and will not be affected by Agenda for Change.

A career in management

In the past the nursing career structure was flat and nurses who wished to become managers had to make a leap from ward manager to deputy director of nursing. There were few middle management posts available. That changed in the late 1990s when the modern matron role was introduced. Now each group of wards or each department has a modern matron role. In some places these are called modern matron, in others head of nursing, in others clinical lead. The posts are all at middle management level.

The modern matron's role is a new one and is not yet well defined. It aims to provide visible managers who have the power to enable and empower staff and improve quality of care. Expectations of educational requirements and experience for modern matrons vary. Normally modern matrons are required to have clinical expertise and to be developing managerial expertise, but increasingly employers require their modern matrons to have a degree. Nurses who are not qualified to degree level may wish to study management at degree level or to combine management modules with clinical modules within a degree in order to become a modern matron. Nurses who are already qualified to degree level may wish to study management at postgraduate certificate or diploma level or at MSc level. It looks likely that modern matrons will be paid on pay band 7 in the Agenda for Change pay bands.

The next rung on the management ladder is deputy or assistant director of nursing. In Hospital and Community Trusts one or more deputy or assistant directors of nursing support the modern matrons and report to the director of nursing. Deputy and director of nursing posts are considered to be senior management roles and are outside the scope of Agenda for Change, which concentrates on clinical grades. At present a deputy director of nursing will earn around £40–46,000 a year depending on responsibilities. Directors of nursing are paid varying salaries. The highest paid director of nursing in England was paid £102,500 in 2003. Nursing directors in acute hospitals tend to be paid more than those working in community settings. The average director of nursing in a Hospital Trust earns around £70–71,000. The average nursing director in a Community (Primary Care) Trust earns around £56,000.

FURTHER EDUCATION AND DEVELOPMENT

All nurses are required to continue their professional development if they are to remain registered as nurses. Nurses are legally required to demonstrate that they have met their professional obligations by practising for 100 days (750 hours) in five years and completing the equivalent of five study days over three years. The NMC produces a useful guide called *The PREP Handbook*, which can be obtained by writing to the NMC or it can downloaded from the NMC Web site (see Chapter 10 for details). Nurses are required to register every three years, to confirm that they have met PREP regulations and to pay a registration fee. At the time of writing the NMC is considering allowing nurses, midwives and health visitors to pay an annual fee.

PAY BANDS

See Table 4.1 for details of the Agenda for Change pay bands.

CAREER OPTIONS

Registered nurses have many career options. They can choose to remain at the bedside caring for patients. They can choose to develop a career in clinical practice, management or education. Nurses have the option to work part-time (see Chapter 5). They can choose to work in hospital, in the community or in practice nursing or the new diagnostic

Table 4.1 Agenda for Change pay bands

Point	Band 1	Band 2	Band 3	Band 4	Band 5	Band 6	Band 7	Band 8			
								Range A	Range B	Range C	Range D
1	10,762	10,975*									
2	11,135										
3	11,508	11,508	11,668*								
4	11,827	11,827									
5	11,768	12,147	12,147*								
6	12,129	12,520									
7	12,490	12,893	12,733*								
8	12,852	13,266	13,266	13,479*							
9	13,316	13,745	13,745								
10	13,832	14,278	14,278	14,278*							
11	14,142		14,598								
12	14,555		15,024	14,811*							
13	15,019		15,504	15,504							
14	15,381		15,877	15,877	15,877*						
15	15,948			16,463	16,516*						
16	16,516			17,049	17,049*						
17	17,032			17,581							
18	17,548			18,114	18,114						
19	18,064			18,647	18,647	18,913*					
20	18,581				19,180						
21	19,200				19,819	19,819*					
22	19,819				20,458						
23	20,387				21,044	20,778*					
24	20,955				21,630	21,630					
25	21,780				22,483	22,483	22,057*				
26	22,710				23,442	23,442	23,442*				
27	23,639					24,401					
28	24,464					25,253	24,827*				
29	25,290					26,106	26,106				
30	26,116					26,958	26,958				
31	27,045					27,917	27,917				
32	28,387					29,302	29,302				
33	29,213						30,155	30,155*			
34	30,142						31,114	31,114*			
35	31,174						32,179	32,179*			

Table 4.1   *Continued*

Point	Band 1	Band 2	Band 3	Band 4	Band 5	Band 6	Band 7	Band 8			
								Range A	Range B	Range C	Range D
36	32,258						33,298	33,298			
37	33,342						34,417	34,417	34,417*		
38	34,684							35,802	35,802*		
39	36,026							37,187	37,187*		
40	37,574							38,786	38,786		
41	38,709							39,958	39,958	39,958*	
42	40,671								41,982	41,982*	
43	42,942								44,326	44,326*	
44	45,213								46,671	46,671	
45	46,451								47,949	47,949	47,949*
46	48,516									50,080	50,080*
47	50,787									52,425	52,425*
48	54,193									55,941	55,941
49	55,742									57,539	57,539
50	58,064										59,937
51	60,903										62,867
52	64,000										66,063
53	67,096										69,260

*Pay rates in italic are special transitional points, which apply only during assimilation to the new system in accordance with the proposed agreement on Agenda for Change.

treatment centres. Chapter 7 provides details of community roles. Nurses can choose to work in the independent sector (see Chapter 9). They can choose to develop in advanced clinical practice (Chapter 8 gives details) and to expand their roles. Nurses who have taken a career break are encouraged to return (see Chapter 5).

5

Returning to nursing after a career break

The NHS, GP surgeries, and the independent sector need more nurses. Last year NHS spending on agency nurses hit record levels. The government plans to recruit an additional 7,000 nurses to the NHS in England every year until 2010. This will be difficult because the NHS workforce is ageing and those nurses who leave because of retirement need replacing. The government's recruitment strategy includes, increasing the number of student nurses, reducing drop-out rates on education programmes, improving recruitment and retention and encouraging nurses to return to nursing.

Most nurses who leave nursing tend to be in their early 30s or late 50s. Many nurses in their early 30s leave nursing to bring up a family. They often find that the costs of childcare and inflexible working patterns make it difficult to balance home and work life.

Many nurses in their late 50s have caring responsibilities or wish to wind down and work on a part-time basis. In the past some NHS Trusts were unsympathetic to such requests and some nurses in this age group left the profession because of this.

Registered nurses are a precious resource and it costs at least £50,000 to educate a registered nurse. Now the government recognises that to have nurses leave the profession is an appalling waste of talent and have introduced initiatives to encourage those who wish to work part-time to stay in nursing and to support nurses who wish to return to work.

WHY RETURN TO NURSING?

Many nurses who take a career break because of caring responsibilities intend to return to nursing but when the opportunity arises for them to return many feel that nursing has changed so much that they will no longer be able to cope. In the past nurses registered for life and a nurse's name remained on the register even if the nurse was not practising. Now the NMC operates a 'live' register. Nurses are required to fulfil practice requirements and must have practised for 100 days (750 hours) in the last five years to meet practice requirements. Nurses, like midwives and health visitors, must also meet continuing education requirements (see Chapter 4) and reregister with the NMC every three years. Nurses who do not fulfil these requirements are not reregistered and their nursing registration is said to have 'lapsed'. Nurses who are not currently on the NMC register cannot practise as registered nurses and must complete a return to practice course and reregister as nurses before they can practise.

AVAILABLE SUPPORT

In 2001 the Department of Health in England and the other UK countries introduced returner packages designed to support nurses who wish to return to practice. They have been successful in helping around 4,000 nurses a year to return to practice. Returner packages differ slightly in each UK country but they share key elements. Each package offers a return to practice course for the nurse who wishes to take up nursing again. The NHS meets the cost of the course. The package also includes financial support for nurses while they complete the return to practice course. Support may include a bursary while taking the course. Some NHS Trusts pay nurses at different pay scales rather than pay a bursary. Some Trusts pay nurses health care assistant salaries, whilst others pay them at the lowest point on the registered nurse pay scale. The package includes help with travel costs and with childcare costs. If you are interested in returning to practice, your local NHS Trust or education consortium will be able to give you details. Many return to practice courses are part-time, so that people with caring responsibilities can complete the course. Some courses are run to fit in with school hours, others have flexible elements so that the core attendance time is between 9.30 am and 2.30 pm and returners can fit individual study time in between other commitments. If you are receiving state benefits any bursary payment may affect your benefits. The New Deal scheme aims to ensure that people returning to work are not worse off than when they are on benefit. Sometimes returning to work means that different types of benefits are paid. Local job centres have specialist New Deal Advisors to consult on such issues.

Return to practice courses

Nurses who are no longer registered are required to successfully complete a return to practice course before they can apply to rejoin the register. A nurse who has been out of practice for a few years but who remains on the register is not required to complete a return to practice course, but many of these nurses prefer to complete a different course, often called a clinical support programme. Many NHS Trusts also prefer nurses who have a break of a few years to complete a clinical support programme.

The purpose of a return to practice programme is to enable the nurse to renew registration and re-enter registered practice with up-to-date competence, current skills and confidence. Most NHS Trusts work with universities to offer a return to practice programme. A typical programme lasts for 15 weeks, and includes 12 days at university updating on the theory of nursing. Many Trusts run a certain number of programmes per year – usually between two and four – and have intake dates. If you are planning to return to practice contact your local NHS Trust early to ensure that you get a place on the appropriate course. Most courses include a written assignment which provides 15–20 credits at level 2 and can be used towards a diploma in nursing.

TYPICAL LEARNING OUTCOMES ON A RETURN TO PRACTICE COURSE

- Gain an understanding of the influence of health and social policies that are relevant to nursing practice.

- Gain an understanding of the requirements of legislation, guidelines, codes of practice and policies.

- Develop an understanding of the current structure and organisation of care, both nationally and locally.

- Develop an understanding of current issues in nursing education and practice.

- Discuss the use of relevant literature and research to inform the practice of nursing.

- Discuss the assessment of need, the design and implementation of interventions, and the evaluation of outcomes in relevant areas of practice, including emergency care.

- Explore the use of appropriate communication and teaching skills.

- Recognise the importance of maintaining and developing professional competence.

Each course includes an element of clinical practice. Nurse returners are normally allocated to a particular ward or department for the whole of their clinical practice. Most NHS Trusts employ a return to practice facilitator or lecturer who is responsible for overseeing the programme. The facilitator arranges a suitable placement for the returner and organises a ward-based or department-based preceptor. Once a clinical placement has been organised, the student negotiates the working arrangements with his or her preceptor. This enables the returner to balance home and work commitments. Some returners arrange to work full days, while others may wish to work half days, or a combination of full and half days.

The nurse returning to practice will achieve his or her individual practice outcomes while working within a clinical setting. The returner is not included in the ward staffing levels and is supernumerary during the course. This helps the nurse to regain confidence and skills without adding to the pressures on a busy ward.

The facilitator and the ward-based preceptor work together to enable the returner to update clinical skills. They also work with the returner to enable him or her to meet individual learning outcomes. When the returner completes the course successfully he or she can apply to register with the NMC. Most nurses (85 per cent) of those who complete return to practice courses apply for posts within the NHS. These are available on a full- or part-time basis. Nurses who have reregistered are normally allocated a preceptor and have four months of supported practice.

Clinical support programmes

Clinical support programmes aim to support nurses returning to clinical practice or those moving to a different area of clinical practice. Many nurses who remain on the register but have taken a career break wish to take part in a clinical support programme. Many NHS Trusts also prefer nurses who have taken a career break to complete such a programme. Sometimes nurses who have been working in a different area of nursing choose to apply for a clinical support programme. A nurse who has worked abroad in a different setting or who has worked in the community for some years may wish to complete a clinical support programme to prepare for working in an acute hospital.

Clinical support programmes vary from one NHS Trust to another. They are usually 12 weeks long and are often individually tailored. Normally such programmes have around eight study days and have expected outcomes.

OUTCOMES OF CLINICAL SUPPORT PROGRAMMES

- Be able to locate key departments within the NHS Trust.

- Be aware of Trust and local policies and procedures.

- Be familiar with Trust and local documentation.

- Have an understanding of the role of the nurse in the changing NHS.

- Have had the opportunity to review and update your clinical practice.

- Be aware of professional opportunities within the NHS Trust.

- Have had the opportunity to reflect and discuss issues that are related to your practice.

- Have had the opportunity and support to determine and achieve your own specific learning objectives.

Each support programme includes an element of clinical practice. Nurses are normally allocated to a particular ward or department for the whole of their clinical practice. The nurse will, like nurses on the return to practice course, have the support of a practice facilitator and a ward-based or department preceptor.

ENROLLED NURSES

Enrolled nursing was introduced in 1943. Enrolled nurses were then known as state enrolled assistant nurses. The assistant was dropped from the title when formal training courses were introduced in the 1960s. Then enrolled nurse training was two years long. In 1992 enrolled nurse training was discontinued and the enrolled nurse register was closed. All nurse education programmes moved to three-year programmes. In 1997 there were 100,000 enrolled nurses working in the UK. There are now around 20,000.

Enrolled nurses who have let their registration lapse can complete a return to practice course and reregister as enrolled or second-level nurses. Many enrolled nurses who return to practice choose to complete a conversion course and upgrade their qualification to first-level registered nurse.

Education options for enrolled nurses

An enrolled nurse's options to upgrade his or her qualification depend on the person's initial qualification. The old enrolled nurse (general) qualification enables the nurse to upgrade to registered nurse (adult branch). The enrolled nurse (mental) qualification enables the nurse to upgrade to registered nurse (mental health).

Enrolled nurses have two options when they wish to upgrade qualifications. They can apply for a distance learning course or a part-time course where they attend university. Distance learning courses are run by universities all over the UK. The RDL learning Web site gives details of current courses. Your local workforce confederation can also supply information (see Chapter 10).

Nurses undertaking a conversion programme must be in full- or part-time employment. Students who work less than 20 hours a week may need to increase their working hours to fulfil course requirements. Students are required to have the equivalent of one year's full-time experience and must have a written letter of support from their manager.

When enrolled nurse training was discontinued there was a huge demand for courses to upgrade qualifications and it could be difficult to obtain funding. Demand has reduced dramatically in recent years. Some enrolled nurses have retired and many who wished to become registered nurses have now done so. Now most NHS Trusts are able to pay the course fees of nurses who wish to upgrade their qualifications. The learning development coordinator at the NHS Trust where you plan to return to work will able to advise you of how to apply for this.

FLEXIBLE WORKING HOURS

In the past some nurses found it difficult to obtain part-time posts or posts with hours that enabled them to balance home and work commitments. In 2000 the government introduced a new policy in the NHS called Improving Working Lives. Every NHS Trust is now expected to offer staff more flexible working conditions, the opportunity to take career breaks and flexible retirement policies that enable staff to reduce hours prior to retirement.

If you wish to return to nursing and to work certain hours your local NHS Trust will be receptive to your request. No NHS trust will be able to guarantee every single person will be able to work exactly the shifts or hours required, as there is a need to balance the needs of the service with needs of staff. NHS Trusts are much more flexible and open to nurses who wish to work flexibly.

CHILDCARE

The NHS is spending £100 million on supporting childcare to help staff to balance work and family life. NHS Strategic Health Authorities are organisations that support and direct NHS Hospital and Community Trusts. Each Strategic Health Authority has developed a childcare strategy.

AN EXAMPLE OF CHILDCARE STRATEGY

- Provide better information about childcare and work life balance to NHS staff in either NHS Trusts or Primary Care Trusts, including GPs and their staff.

- Increase access to a variety of good quality, flexible and affordable childcare, through the development of new provision for all age groups and via partnerships.

- Make childcare more affordable through tax effective payment schemes, increase take up of Child Tax Credit and the childcare element of Working Tax Credit.

- Double the amount of NHS childcare provision across the sector.

- Open access to all provision in the sector to all NHS staff.

- Work in partnership with Local Authorities, Early Years Development and Childcare Partnerships and Children's Information Services.

- Support the Improving Working Lives Standard on Childcare.

Many NHS Trusts now operate subsidised day nurseries for the children of staff. These nurseries increasingly operate at hours to suit parents who are working shifts. There are plans to increase the number of nursery places. The NHS is also setting up a national NHS childminding network. Many parents, especially those who work part-time during school hours, face particular problems in finding childcare during school holidays. Almost all NHS Trusts now run holiday play schemes offering childcare and activities for school-age children during the holidays. These schemes are very popular and there are plans to increase them.

Individual NHS Trusts have now appointed childcare coordinators to help parents. The childcare coordinator can help by:

- providing information about affordable, good quality, flexible childcare;

- providing information and help with Working Tax Credit, which contains a childcare element that can form an important source of help with childcare fees for low- to middle-income one- or two-parent families who are working more than 16 hours a week and who meet the eligibility criteria;

- providing information and help with Child Tax Credit for parents earning up to £58,000 a year as a household, who are also entitled to up to £545 a year (more if the child is under a year old);

■ supporting staff on and returning from maternity leave;

■ developing local childcare to meet needs;

■ promoting family friendly working practices.

TAKING THE PLUNGE

Many nurses lose confidence when they take a break from nursing. They feel that they have forgotten all their skills and that nursing has changed beyond recognition since they left. Nurses who are considering returning to nursing bring a great deal back into nursing. They bring maturity and life experience. The nurse who is a parent can understand and empathise with the parent of a sick child. The nurse who has supported her own parents can understand the anxieties of adults whose parents are ill and require care in hospital.

Many things in nursing have changed but the nature of nursing has not. Patients still require nurses who are caring and kind and who will listen to them and explain treatments. Although some techniques have changed, the essence of nursing and the caring role have not.

It is difficult and a little intimidating to consider a return to nursing. If you have been caring for children at home you must reorganise your life so that you can fit household tasks into a shorter time. You also have to learn how to prioritise at home and to delegate some household tasks to the rest of your family. The benefit of returning to nursing is that you will once again be able to make a difference to people's lives and enjoy a fulfilling career.

It is natural to feel nervous and uncertain when returning to work but many of the staff you are working with will have been in the same position themselves. You will find colleagues supportive and helpful. Returning to nursing can appear daunting but around 4,000 nurses successfully return each year. Some choose to return to full-time work, others work part-time. Most were unaware of the levels of support that are now available and say that had they been aware of this they would have returned sooner.

TOP TIPS

■ Check whether you are required to complete a return to practice course.

■ Contact your local NHS Trust or NHS confederation for details of courses.

■ Prepare for your interview.

■ Work out how you will manage to balance work and home.

■ Consider working part-time initially – it is easy to increase hours as you get back into the swing of working.

■ Use the childcare coordinator for advice and support.

6

International nurses working in the UK

In 2003 for the first time ever the number of international nurses joining the NMC register exceeded the number educated in the UK. In 2003 more than 16,000 nurses educated outside the UK joined the NMC register. Most of these (93 per cent) came from outside the EU. Among the main non-EU groups were nurses from the Philippines (7,000) South Africa (2,000) and Australia (1,000).

Avoiding the pitfalls

Many international nurses are attracted to working in the UK because of familiar culture and language, educational opportunities and comparatively high salaries. Although the cost of living in the UK is much higher than in some other countries nurses from many countries can earn 10 or 15 times as much here as at home.

Some unscrupulous employers and agencies prey on international nurses' desires to work in the UK. Some nurses are told that it is not possible to become registered in the UK without using an agency. Some nurses are worried about registering in an unfamiliar and at times confusing system and choose to pay agencies. Agencies can charge nurses enormous amounts of money – sums of £3,000, representing well over a year's salary in the nurse's home country, have been reported. If you are an international nurse wishing to work in the UK, this chapter aims to guide you through the process of applying to work here without using such agencies.

There have also been reports of nurses being recruited who were promised help to register as a nurse in the UK only to find that when they arrived they were not given the support needed to register. This chapter aims to help you understand how to decide if job offers are really offering you the right level of support to register.

QUALIFICATIONS REQUIRED TO REGISTER IN THE UK

In the UK only first-level nurses and midwives can register. Many countries have training programmes leading to qualifications that are recordable in their own country but do not meet EU standards. Examples of qualifications that are not recognisable are:

- enrolled nurse;

- practical nurse (licensed or registered);

- vocational nurse;

- community nurse;

- state certified nurse;

- mothercraft nurse.

EU STANDARDS

The countries of the UK, like other European countries, are obliged by law to meet European directives on nurse education. These directives state that nurses must complete education programmes that are three years long and have 4,600 hours of education and training. Many countries have shorter education programmes (as the UK once did before enrolled nurse education was discontinued). Nurses who have qualifications that do not meet EU standards cannot apply to join the register in the UK.

Some of the qualifications from other countries that do not meet these standards are:

- registered geriatric nurse (Australia);

- mothercraft nurse (Australia);

- nurse aide (Canada);

- qualified registered nurse – QRN (Ghana);

- Beyhari nurse (Iran);

- practical nurse certificate holder (Israel);

- technical Baccalaureate certificate holder (Lebanon);

- nurse midwife technician (Malawi);

- community care nurse (New Zealand);

- Karitane nurse (New Zealand);

- Plunkett nurse (New Zealand);

- assistant nurse certificate holder (Romania);

- staff nurse (South Africa);

- medical assistant certificate holder (USA);

- licensed practical nurse (USA);

- licensed vocational nurse (USA).

Nurses who have such qualifications are required to retrain in the UK if they wish to register to work as a nurse here. However, in order to apply for a UK registration programme nurses must meet residency requirements (see Chapter 2). It is not normally possible for nurses to come to the UK and begin retraining without meeting these requirements.

LANGUAGE REQUIREMENTS

The NMC has the right to ask any nurse trained outside the EU to take a language test. In practice the NMC normally requires nurses who were educated in countries where English is not the first language to take the International English Language Testing System (IELTS) test. These are administered by the British Council (see Chapter 10 for contact details).

APPLYING TO THE NMC

The NMC is responsible for registering all nurses working in the UK. It is not possible to work as a registered nurse without active NMC registration.

In order to register you need to obtain an information pack. This can be done either by writing to the NMC and asking for one to be posted or by downloading one from the NMC Web site. The NMC site can be very busy and downloading can take some time. The application pack contains forms and information about what you need to send to the NMC. To register you will need to supply:

■ registration certificate, birth certificate, copies of diplomas;

■ two references from employers (agencies are not acceptable);

■ a transcript of your training from your training provider giving details of how much practical training and theoretical education you have received;

■ a signed form from the regulator in your country to demonstrate that your registration is effective and that there are no outstanding disciplinary issues.

If you wish to proceed you must complete the application pack and send the relevant documents and a fee of £117 to the NMC. The NMC uses the information you have supplied to assess your application.

Assessment of the application

Each application is investigated in order to:

■ assess that the applicant is established as a first-level nurse in his or her country of training and that he or she is of a good standing in that country and in any other country in which he or she might be registered;

EUROPEAN EXPANSION

In May 2004 10 new countries joined the EU. These were Cyprus, Czech Republic, Estonia, Hungary, Latvia, Lithuania, Malta, Poland, Slovakia and Slovenia. In theory, nurses registered within the EU can come to work as registered nurses in the UK. In practice, nurses who wish to work as registered nurses in the EU must meet EU standards. Some EU countries, such as Poland, Estonia and Slovakia, do not yet meet those standards. The NMC will approve all applicants from the expanded EU countries until their education programmes meet EU standards. New programmes that are being run at present in expanded EU countries now meet EU standards however many registered practitioners have undertaken programmes that do not meet current standards. In Poland, for example, it was possible to register as a nurse with only six months' training up to 1990. It seems likely in the short term that the NMC will adopt similar procedures to deal with applications from countries in the expanded EU as it already has in place for international nurses.

Many nurses from Eastern Europe are expected to find working in the UK attractive and growing numbers are predicted to enter the UK job market over the next five years. The NMC Web site provides up-to-date details of the registration process for nurses from the expanded EU.

EDUCATION AND PRACTICE OPPORTUNITIES

Many nurses are attracted to working in the UK. UK nursing offers nurses education and practice opportunities that they may not be able to obtain at home. It also offers the opportunity to travel and to work in a completely different culture. Some nurses choose to work in the UK for a short time and then to return home, others choose to make their home in the UK. There are opportunities for international nurses to develop professionally.

TOP TIPS

- Beware of agencies charging high fees and making extravagant promises.

- Obtain an application pack from the NMC before travelling to the UK.

- Ensure that you provide the documents and information required to avoid delays.

- Await your decision letter before seeking a supervised placement.

- Consider looking outside London for a supervised placement.

- If your placing is in the independent sector check that it has been approved by the NMC.

- Check your contract carefully to ensure that you are aware of the maximum number of hours you are required to work.

- Join a professional organisation (see Chapter 10) as these are a good source of support and advice.

7

Community nursing

When people think of nursing the image that comes to mind is of a nurse working in a busy hospital. This is often a fairly accurate image as most nurses work in hospital settings with only 13 per cent of NHS nurses working in community settings. However, the image of nursing as a hospital-based profession is changing. Community nursing is growing more rapidly than hospital nursing. Community nursing offers patients the opportunity to have care delivered closer to home and sometimes in the home. It offers nurses the potential to develop practice in new ways. Community nursing is made up of different types of nursing and different levels within each type. This chapter aims to give you an insight into community nursing.

DISTRICT NURSING

Nurses of all grades are employed as district nurses. There are posts available for senior staff nurses, junior sisters, and more senior grades as qualified district nurses. Normally registered nurses are required to have at least one year's post-registration experience before they will be considered for a post in community nursing. This is because district nurses often work on their own and are required to have some experience before they can begin their career working in the community. Nurses considering working in district nursing are normally required to have experience of working with older people and experience of medical and surgical nursing. It is helpful if nurses have some experience of working in palliative care.

The district nurse's role is varied. District nurses care for patients in a variety of settings. They may provide care in the patient's own home, in a residential care home, in a health centre, or in a clinic in a community hospital. Patients may include frail older people who would be unable to live at home without the care of district nurses, people who have been discharged from hospital recently who require short periods of care and people who require ongoing care. Health promotion is an important part of the district nurse's role.

THE ROLE OF THE DISTRICT NURSE

- Accept referrals from GPs and hospital staff.

- Assess, manage and plan the care of patients.

- Assess the need for registered nursing care.

- Provide support to patients and their families and carers and teach care-giving skills.

- Work with patients, families, carers and other professionals.

- Ensure that patients, families and carers understand how treatment and medicine are given.

- Monitor patients, identify problems and refer to appropriate organisations when necessary.

- Check temperature, blood pressure and pulse readings, administer drugs and injections, set up drips, clean and dress wounds, take blood and urine samples.

- Prescribe medicines and aids that the patient requires.

- Work with other services to ensure that the patient receives high quality care.

District nurses normally wear uniforms. Working hours vary, core hours are 8.00 am until 4.00 pm and the bulk of district nursing work is carried out within these hours. District nurses provide care seven days a week and many work weekends and late at night.

Education programmes

Nurses who wish to qualify as district nurses and to progress in their career beyond junior sister level are required to have specialist qualifications in district nursing. The minimum qualification is now a BSc Honours in District Nursing. This is a one-year programme that comprises 50 per cent theory and 50 per cent practice. Part-time courses are available and these are two years long. The educational component is delivered at universities throughout the UK. Nurses must have a diploma in nursing or must be able to demonstrate that they have obtained 120 credits at level 2 in order to start the programme.

Nurses who have relevant experience at degree level (level 3) can use the APEL and APL programme to gain credit for previous study (see page 45 for details) and in such circumstances can qualify in a shorter time. Nurses who already have degrees in nursing can apply to study district nursing at Master's degree level. If the nurse is successful he or she will obtain a postgraduate diploma in district nursing. This can be 'topped up' to a Master's degree by doing a research project.

Sponsorship

Registered nurses who wish to study district nursing can obtain sponsorships to do so. Normally such nurses are working in the NHS as experienced staff nurses and are seconded to the course on the midpoint of a senior staff nurse salary. This means that the staff nurse receives his or her normal salary while studying. Sometimes nurses who are working at junior sister grade suffer some loss of salary under such arrangements. Sometimes special consideration is given to nurses at junior sister or sister grade and it is possible to second the nurse on a higher salary grade. Course fees are met by the NHS.

University courses normally begin in September and nurses are advised to apply at least six months in advance. Details of sponsorship opportunities are advertised in the nursing press and locally via NHS recruitment bulletins. The nurse must apply for the course, be accepted onto the course and then have an interview with the local Primary Care Trust who are sponsoring the place.

TOP TIPS FOR DISTRICT NURSING

■ Find out as much as you can about district nursing before applying.

■ If possible gain experience working in the community as a district staff nurse.

■ Gain relevant experience and qualifications for example palliative care, care of older people, wound care.

■ Read specialist journals to increase your knowledge.

■ Ensure that you have the appropriate qualifications to apply.

■ Apply early for a place.

■ Prepare for the interview.

HEALTH VISITING

Health visiting is very different from district nursing. The prime role of the health visitor is health promotion. Health visitors are registered nurses who have specialist education in community health care. It is possible to obtain a post as a registered nurse on the health visiting team. These posts are available for junior staff nurses who can gain promotion to senior staff nurse or junior sister grade. Nurses have a caseload and are supervised by the health visitor. The work, like health visiting has four key components. These are:

■ providing health advice;

■ providing health education;

■ supporting parents;

■ checking on child health and development.

Specialist health visitors who work with older people have similar roles.

The health visitor works with all age groups, however, most health visitors work with families with pre-school children. Some health visitors work with older people. The role of the health visitor is changing rapidly. The main responsibilities of the health visitor are outlined below.

THE ROLE OF THE HEALTH VISITOR

■ Lead teams of health professionals.

■ Work with families in helping them to develop parenting skills.

■ Support families who have a child with special needs.

■ Run parenting groups.

■ Visit families at home, support, advise and inform parents.

■ Deliver child health programmes.

■ Support and work with families where children have chronic illness.

■ Support and work with families when children develop serious or life-threatening illness.

■ Support government schemes such as Sure Start, aimed to reduce child poverty.

■ Work strategically within the Primary Care Trusts to identify health needs of neighbourhoods, and special groups such as the homeless, and develop local health plans.

■ Manage and lead teams delivering local health plans.

- Work with local communities to help them identify and tackle their own health needs.

- Encourage and enable disadvantaged people and communities to develop individual and community health plans.

- Provide health improvement programmes to target accident, cancer, mental health, coronary heart disease and stroke victims.

The health visitor is normally paid a minimum of a sister's salary. This is likely to be band 7 in the Agenda for Change pay bands. There are opportunities for health visitors to manage a team of health visitors or to become an assistant director within a Primary Care Trust. Health visitors may also wish to work in education in either a practice setting or within the university sector.

Health visitors generally work from 9.00 pm to 5.00 pm Monday to Friday and do not wear uniforms. The role often involves lots of travel during the working day.

Education programmes

Health visitors are required to have a specialist post registration qualification in health visiting before they can practise as health visitors. The minimum qualification for a health visitor is now a BSc Honours in Health Visiting. This is a one-year programme that comprises 50 per cent theory and 50 per cent practice. Part-time courses are available and these are two years long. The entry requirements are similar to those for district nursing though health visitors are required to have experience of working with children. Health visiting programmes are available at postgraduate diploma level for nurses who have degrees.

Sponsorship

The procedure for sponsorship is the same as for district nursing.

PRACTICE NURSING

Practice nursing is slightly different from district nursing and health visiting because practice nurses, unlike district nurses and health visitors, do not normally work for Primary Care Trusts. They are usually employed by GPs. GPs are not required to pay NHS salary scales though in practice most do because they wish to attract high quality staff. The Royal College of Nursing (RCN) produces guidance on practice nurse salary scales. This states that practice nurses who work under the supervision of senior practice nurses may be paid on band 5. It states that most practice nurses will be paid on band 6 and nurse practitioners should be paid on band 7 or possibly band 8.

Practice nurses work in GP practices and assess, screen, treat babies, children and adults (including older people) and educate. The practice role varies enormously, encompassing treatment of minor illness to chronic disease management. In each case, the exact role depends on the skill levels of the practice nurse and the expectations of the GP. Some practice nurses work autonomously as nurse practitioners (see Chapter 8), while others have more limited roles.

THE ROLE OF THE PRACTICE NURSE

- Administer injections and vaccinations to babies and children.

- Administer travel immunisations and provide travel health care advice.

- Advise patients about medical and nursing needs.

- Provide advice, information and often treatment on a range of health conditions and minor ailments.

- Refer patients to doctors in the practice when necessary.

- Refer patients to nurse specialists such as continence advisers and diabetes nurse specialists.

- Perform investigations such as testing urine, checking weight, blood pressure, carrying out pregnancy tests.

- Perform minor operations such as cryosurgery to remove warts.

- Conduct first-registration checks.

- Set up and run clinics for chronic disease management such as asthma, diabetes and skin problems.

- Promote health by running well woman and well man clinics.

- Run smoking cessation clinics.

- Give contraceptive advice and fit contraceptive devices.

- Provide cervical smear and pregnancy tests.

- Take blood and urine samples, other specimens and swabs.

- Perform procedures such as ear syringing, eye washing, applying and removing dressings, removing sutures and treating wounds, etc.

- Offer information and advice in areas such as blood pressure, weight control, heart conditions, etc.

- Offer first aid and emergency treatment, as required.

- Re-stock and maintain clinical areas and consulting rooms.

- Maintain records of consultations and treatments and record these in patients' notes.

- Update/amend the clinical computer system with details of patients and treatments.

- Work with doctors, nurse specialists, district nurses, health visitors and others as a team member.

- Liaise with other practice nurses, GPs, reception and office staff.

The practice nurse may be paid at senior staff nurse, junior sister, sister or nurse specialist level. This depends on the practice nurse's role and responsibilities. Practice nurses normally work set hours which are negotiated with the employer. The practice nurse normally works Monday to Friday but if the doctor's surgery opens on a Saturday the nurse may be required to work then. Many practices now employ several practice nurses and such duties are normally shared on a rota basis. Practice hours are often from 8.00 am or 9.00 am to 7.00 pm and some nurses choose to work over three or four days while others work over five days. There are lots of opportunities for part-time working within GP practices. Some practice nurses wear a uniform, others do not. This depends on the type of work being carried out and what is 'normal' within a particular surgery. The RCN recommends that employers provide practice nurses with a uniform.

Education programmes

There are no requirements for practice nurses to have formal educational qualifications in order to work as a practice nurse. However, as practice nursing is changing and the practice nurse is becoming responsible for working independently and seeing, treating and managing individual patients and groups of patients with chronic diseases, many practice nurses are choosing to study for specialist qualifications. There are two relevant qualifications. These are the BSc Honours in Practice Nursing and the BSc Honours Nurse Practitioner. Both courses are available on a full- or part-time basis. The full-time course takes one year and the part-time course two years. Diploma level qualifications are required for both BSc courses. GP practices are small organisations and at most there are only a handful of practice nurses employed so it is difficult for nurses to study full-time. Many practice nurses choose to study part-time so that they can combine work and study. Nurses who have degrees can study practice nursing or the nurse practitioner programme at Master's level.

Sponsorship

The procedure for sponsorship is the same as for district nursing. If a nurse chooses to study part-time the GP employer is paid an allowance to enable a replacement to be paid while the nurse is studying. The nurse receives either an E grade salary or in some circumstances normal salary while studying.

SPECIALIST COMMUNITY PRACTICE

Nurses who specialise in children's nursing or in learning disability nursing also have an important role to play in the community. There are education programmes to enable these nurses to obtain specialist qualifications in community practice. These are the BSc Honours in Community Learning Disability Nursing and the BSc Honours in Community Children's Nursing. Nurses require diploma level qualifications and normally two years' experience as a registered nurse to obtain a place on these courses. They are run on a one-year full-time or two-year part-time basis. Nurses who have degrees can study at Master's level and obtain a postgraduate diploma. Sponsorship is available on the same basis as for district nursing degree courses.

SCHOOL NURSING

School nurses are usually employed by Primary Care Trusts, however many independent schools also employ school nurses. The roles are different.

The school nurse working for the Primary Care Trust focuses on the needs of individual children, their parents and families and the needs of all school-aged children within the primary care trust. School nurses are required to have qualifications in adult or children's nursing and at least two years' experience. Most posts are paid at sister pay grade though this varies from area to area. Some posts are full-time, but many are part-time or for term-time only. (Term-time posts are very popular with nurses who are parents of school-age children.)

Each school nurse has his or her own caseload. The size of the caseload depends upon the number of children in a particular area or the mixture of types of school. The school nurse is often responsible for a number of schools and there might be a mixture of primary and secondary schools. If the school nurse is responsible for schools in a deprived inner city area or schools where large numbers of children with special needs are educated he or she will have a smaller caseload than a school nurse in a well-to-do area.

THE ROLE OF THE SCHOOL NURSE

■ Assess a child when he or she starts school, checking health, height, weight, vision, hearing and development.

■ Advise children and families about health promotion, such as diet and exercise.

■ Carry out immunisation programmes.

■ Protect children at risk of abuse by early detection, prevention and care of children.

■ Train and educate school staff in caring for children with chronic diseases such as asthma and epilepsy.

■ Provide specialist advice, such as contraception advice, to children in secondary schools on a drop-in basis or as part of their education.

■ Provide support and advice for parents and staff on childhood illness.

■ Provide support and advice for parents and staff on communicable diseases and infections.

■ Provide nursing care, support and advice for children in special schools.

■ Provide nursing care, support and advice for children with special needs, their parents, other parents and school staff when these children are cared for in mainstream schools.

■ Refer children to doctors, nurse specialists and other professionals.

■ Work with other professionals as a member of the team.

The school nurse working in an independent school combines a nursing and health promotion role with pastoral care. Sometimes children in independent schools are boarders and live in the school in term-time because parents are working abroad. The nurse working in an independent school is only responsible for the children in that particular school whereas the nurse working in a Primary Care Trust may have a strategic role in addition to the nursing and health promotion roles.

Education programmes

School nursing is now considered to be an area of specialist practice. Education programmes are now at a minimum of degree level. Educational programmes, like those for all other forms of specialist practice, are available on a one-year full-time or two-year part-time basis. Nurses are required to have diploma qualifications for degree programmes and degrees if they wish to obtain a postgraduate diploma. Sponsorship is available on the same basis as for district nursing programmes.

COMMUNITY MENTAL HEALTH NURSING

Community mental health nurses are often referred to as community psychiatric nurses (CPNs). CPNs work with GPs, psychiatrists, social workers and other health professionals to plan and deliver care for people suffering from mental illness. CPNs work with patients in the patients' homes and in residential units. They provide GPs with advice and support and assist them in caring for people with mental health problems. Approximately one person in six will suffer a mental health related problem at some time in their life. Many are reactions to normal life events. eg bereavement or marital breakdown. Some people have complex ongoing mental health problems and the CPNs role is to work with medical staff to ensure that the person receives the most effective modern treatment. Some patients have severe mental illness. CPNs aim to improve these patients' functioning and quality of life, ensuring that a plan of care is maintained to reduce the need for hospital admission. When admission is necessary CPN support enables the earliest possible return home.

CPNs are paid at senior sister or charge nurse rate. Although 10 per cent of all nurses are male a high proportion of men are attracted to mental health nursing.

THE ROLE OF THE COMMUNITY MENTAL HEALTH NURSE

- Assess new patients' behaviour and psychological needs.

- Identify if and when a patient is at risk of harming him- or herself or others and taking appropriate action.

- Assign members of the community mental health nursing team to care for patients.

- Supervise, teach and support members of the community mental health team.

- Coordinate the care of patients in the community.

- Visit patients in their home to monitor progress.

- Support families in caring for relatives with mental health needs.

- Support staff in care homes in caring for people with mental health needs.

- Work with patients, relatives and fellow professionals in the community treatment team to agree care plans.

- Administer medication by injection.

The CPN manages a team of nurses and there are opportunities for registered nurses with mental health qualifications to join the community nursing team. Nurses are paid at staff nurse or junior sister rate. Increasingly mental health nurses who seek more senior posts at sister or charge nurse level or above are required to have a specialist qualification in community mental health nursing.

Education programmes

Mental health nursing is now considered to be an area of specialist practice. Education programmes are now at a minimum of degree level. Educational programmes, like those for all other forms of specialist practice, are available on a one-year full-time or two-year part-time basis. Nurses are required to have diploma qualifications for degree programmes and degrees if they wish to obtain a postgraduate diploma. Sponsorship is available on the same basis as for district nursing programmes.

VARIETY IN COMMUNITY NURSING

Community nursing is varied. There are opportunities for nurses from all branches of nursing to provide care and support in different settings. There are opportunities for nurses to develop a career in clinical practice or management in all of the branches of nursing and to develop within specialist areas of practice.

8

Advanced clinical practice

Nursing is changing. In the past the nurse's role was not that of an independent practitioner – nurses, unlike midwives, could not care for an individual patient or a group of patients independently of doctors. Now though, nurses are developing the skills and knowledge to examine, diagnose, treat, advise and support patients. In the past many experienced nurses found the limitations of their role irritating. An experienced nurse with the right level of skills could examine a patient and decide what was wrong but often needed to consult a doctor in order to get the authority to treat the patient or to obtain medicines required. That is now changing and nursing is beginning to develop advanced practice roles.

What is advanced clinical practice?

Nurse specialists and nurse practitioners began developing advanced clinical practice in hospital and community settings some years ago but there were barriers to these developments. One of the barriers was the lack of official recognition of these new roles. In 1997 the Chief Nurse at the Department of Health published a document called *Liberating the talents* that acknowledged and began to define advanced clinical practice.

NEW ROLES FOR NURSES

NEW ROLES

■ Order diagnostic investigations such as pathology tests and x-rays.

■ Make and receive referrals direct to, say, a therapist or pain consultant.

■ Admit and discharge patients for specified conditions and within agreed protocols.

■ Manage patient caseloads for, say, diabetes or rheumatology.

■ Run clinics for, say, ophthalmology or dermatology.

■ Prescribe medicines or treatments.

■ Carry out a wide range of resuscitation procedures including defibrillation.

■ Perform minor surgery and outpatient procedures.

■ Triage patients using the latest information technology to the most appropriate effect.

■ Take the lead in the way local health services are organised and the way that they are run.

Nurses practising at advanced level have increased ability to make judgements about a patient's condition. They have increased discretion about treatment and increased ability to make decisions about treatment and care. They are responsible for developing their own clinical practice and supporting other nurses in developing their practice. They are leaders who are developing better services for patients at local and national level.

What roles are available?

There are many roles available in advanced clinical practice. Some of these roles involve working with medical, nursing and therapy staff and advising them how to care for patients with specialist needs. Some of the roles involve seeing, treating and discharging patients from an episode of care. Some involve working with medical staff and sharing the care of a patient with a particular condition. There are advanced practice roles available in GP practices, in hospitals and in community settings. The main advanced practice roles are those of nurse practitioner, clinical nurse specialist and nurse consultant.

What education and experience is required?

At present the titles nurse practitioner, clinical nurse specialist and nurse consultant are not protected in law and any nurse or any employer could call a nurse a nurse practitioner or any other title implying that a nurse is practising at advanced level. This situation is set to change. The NMC is currently consulting nurses and their professional organisations. The aim is to decide what core skills and what education a nurse requires to practise at advanced level. When this is decided it seems likely that in the countries of the UK, as in other countries, specialist titles such as nurse practitioner and nurse specialist will be protected by law.

WORKING AS A NURSE PRACTITIONER

The nurse practitioner's role has been developing over the last 20 years. The nurse practitioner has the ability to see patients, diagnose conditions and to treat the person for those conditions. Nurse practitioners differ from most other nurses because they can work independently, examine, investigate, diagnose, treat and discharge patients independently.

ASPECTS OF THE NURSE PRACTITIONER'S ROLE

- Assess, diagnose and treat patients.
- Order and interpret investigations.
- Refer patients to other professionals.

- Work independently and be accountable for decisions.

- Work with patients to promote health and prevent disease.

- Work with patients who have chronic diseases to reduce complications.

- Review prescribed medicines and change medicines when necessary.

- Prescribe medicines when necessary.

- Run clinics to manage disease.

- Run health promotion clinics.

Nurse practitioners work in hospitals, minor injury centres, walk-in centres, GP surgeries and in community settings. The nurse practitioner role is still developing and varies according to the setting and the skills of the nurses delivering the service. The following case histories illustrate these differences.

Case history: Emergency nurse practitioner

Andy Parrott is a senior emergency nurse practitioner at Homerton Hospital. He qualified in 1984.

I worked in accident and emergency (A&E) when I first qualified and then went [to gain] some experience on the wards. I returned to A&E and worked for a year with the major injuries unit at Birmingham Accident Unit. I learnt how to work with people who had suffered major trauma and worked on the roadside recovery unit. This involved emergency treatment of people following car accidents.

In 1995 I went to work in the minor injury unit at Homerton Hospital. I received special training from a medical consultant. I work independently as a nurse practitioner with GP support. I also teach nurse practitioners on the nurse practitioner course at Middlesex University.

I've completed the accident and emergency course, the advanced nurse practitioner course, an advanced trauma nursing course, advanced life support and have a BSc Honours Nurse Practitioner degree.

The best thing about being an emergency nurse practitioner is that I am my own boss. I work as part of a team but I am responsible for seeing, diagnosing, treating and discharging patients.

I believe that nurse practitioners are underpaid given their level of skills. There's a growing recognition that experienced nurse practitioners are working to the same level as medical staff and are often more experienced.

Case history: Nurse practitioner general practice

Lorna Gibson works as a nurse practitioner in a GP surgery.

I worked as a sister in intensive care for years. When I had my children I decided to do something different. I did a family planning course and worked as a family planning nurse in the afternoons and evenings. I was offered a post running a well woman clinic in a GP practice. As the children grew older I increased my hours and worked as a practice nurse. In those days it was difficult. I had to search for courses. I did an asthma diploma and courses in cancer screening and diabetes. When the nurse practitioner degree was introduced I did my BSc Honours Nurse Practitioner degree part-time. Then I was given the opportunity to work with an experienced nurse practitioner on a part-time basis so I gained new skills.

I completed my master's degree in nursing in 2000. I've just completed my nurse prescribing course. Now I see patients who are unwell. The patient might have an acute illness or the worsening of a chronic condition. I assess the patient, order investigations if needed, diagnose and prescribe medicines if these are needed. I also run a number of clinics such as the asthma and diabetes clinics.

It's very rewarding. I work independently and have developed confidence in my practice. I am able to care for the whole person and to treat patients and improve care.

I also teach and work with practice nurse and nurse practitioner students allocated to the practice.

Pay and conditions

It is predicted that nurse practitioners who work in hospitals and NHS Community Trusts will be paid at Agenda for Change band 7 or possibly band 8 in some circumstances. They will have the same conditions as other NHS staff (see pages 39–40 and 50–51 for details).

It is not yet clear if nurse practitioners working in general practice will be paid on Agenda for Change pay scales. It is clear though that even if GPs are not compelled to pay according to Agenda for Change pay scales these will influence pay rates within general practice.

WORKING AS A CLINICAL NURSE SPECIALIST

Clinical nurse specialist roles were introduced in hospitals around 25 years ago. Clinical nurse specialists now work in hospital and community settings. The role varies from one NHS Trust to another – the level of expertise required; the level of clinical freedom available, and the salary paid for the role all vary enormously.

Some clinical nurse specialists have a teaching and advisory role. They advise medical and nursing staff about caring for patients with particular conditions. They also teach nurses and other professionals how to care for people with particular conditions. Some clinical nurse specialists combine the teaching and advisory roles with clinical practice. The clinical nurse specialist who specialises in heart disease may see patients in hospital, discuss treatment with the patient and with nurses and other professionals and see the patient in an outpatient clinic.

Pay and conditions

It is predicted that clinical nurse specialists will be paid at Agenda for Change band 7 or possibly band 8 in some circumstances. They will have the same conditions as other NHS staff (see pages 39–40 and 50–51 for details).

WORKING AS A NURSE CONSULTANT

In the autumn of 1999 Prime Minister Tony Blair announced that the Department of Health would develop a new nursing role: 'Nurse consultants who would carry the same status within their profession as medical consultants have within their profession'.

The first nurse consultants were appointed in 1999. All nurse consultant posts had to be approved by the Department of Health until 2003 when Strategic Health Authorities took on this role. There are now nurse consultants who specialise in caring for people who have a particular disease, such as diabetes. There are also nurse consultants who care for particular groups of people, such as older people or people with mental health needs.

There are four components to the nurse consultant's role.

THE ROLE OF THE NURSE CONSULTANT

▓   Work with patients in clinical practice.

▓   Work in education and training.

▓   Develop strategy.

▓   Carry out research.

The nurse consultant is required to spend at least 50 per cent of his or her time working with patients and to divide his or her remaining time between the remaining activities. The nurse consultant's role is that of a 'maxi nurse' not a 'mini doctor'.

Case history: Nurse consultant

Jackie Tapping works as a nurse consultant in intermediate care with Sutton and Merton Primary Care Trust. Intermediate care enables people who have left hospital to continue their rehabilitation. It can also provide care in the patient's home to prevent the need for hospital admission.

I qualified as a general nurse and went straight in to health visitor training. I spent 14 years with two Area Health Authorities caring for the under fives and older people. This role fitted well with working and bringing up three children. Then I decided on a career change! I joined the practice of one of the GPs I had worked for as a health visitor. After two years I was sponsored and did the nurse practitioner training at the RCN. I gained the Nurse Practitioner Diploma and BSc Honours degree in Health Studies.

I worked as a nurse practitioner for six years. I was made redundant in 1998 and became a team leader in intermediate care. I found that some patients with respiratory problems needed frequent intermediate care. I set up a programme to improve diagnosis treatment and ongoing care of patients with respiratory disease.

I went to work at St George's Hospital, London for two years to learn more about respiratory disease. I completed the asthma and chronic obstructive pulmonary disease diploma. I returned to the PCT developed patient care pathways to improve care of patients with respiratory disease.

The PCT considered that intermediate care was an important area of work and decided to introduce a nurse consultant post. I applied and was appointed in 2001. The role is challenging but very rewarding. The challenge has been in overcoming some degree of confusion at both nursing and clinical level in establishing just what the role entails, a confusion that I sometimes share!

The rewards have been in breaking new ground. My post allows me to develop clinical practice and strategy.

I spend half my time in advanced practice in contact with patients and nurses, practising and educating. Recently I worked with another nurse consultant in accident and emergency assessing and treating patients with minor illness. This helped to reduce waiting times. It also enabled us to educate patients about when to use accident and emergency and when to use other services and to reduce the number of patients who come to A&E unnecessarily. We've used this work to develop generic nurse practitioner training in hospitals and community settings.

I also work to change services and the way we deliver services. I review guidelines and work on creating care pathways and protocols to guide staff in delivering care. I work on quality issues such as the Department of Health initiative Essence of Care within the PCT.

I am also an honorary nurse lecturer at Kingston University. My work at the university has included redesigning some courses and training packages. I teach at the university and advise on my speciality.

I'm also working with the PCT to develop intermediate care. We're working on introducing a generic worker role across areas of the PCT.

The road to nurse consultancy is exciting and challenging, it would be misleading to suggest it has been easy, long periods of study combined with working at a career involving high stress levels, together with bringing up a family often comes with a cost. Would I change anything? The answer has to be no, nursing for me has been the most fantastic career. Being a nurse consultant enables me to combine patient care, which is paramount to those of us who value our clinical role with that of making a difference in developing services and teaching.

Pay and conditions

It is predicted that nurse consultants who work in hospitals and NHS Community Trusts will be paid at Agenda for Change band 8. There are four subdivisions of band 8: bands 8a to 8d. Those who have greater responsibilities and higher education and skill levels will be paid on bands 8b and 8c. They will have the same conditions as other NHS staff (see pages 39–40 and 50–51 for details).

EDUCATION AND TRAINING FOR ADVANCED PRACTICE

At present the nursing profession is in the process of agreeing standards for advanced practice. The introduction of Agenda for Change will hasten this process. Agenda for Change requires that all employers rewrite job descriptions and specify the knowledge and skills required for each post within the health service. This process is linked to Agenda for Change and in the future salaries will be related to the knowledge and skills staff at all levels of practice require to carry out their work.

It is currently possible to work as a nurse practitioner without having a degree or relevant courses in the area of practice where you work. However, it is advisable for nurses working as nurse practitioners to gain solid experience in the area where they work before accepting a nurse practitioner post. Relevant educational courses enable the nurse to develop as an advanced practitioner. The courses required vary according to where the nurse is practising. A nurse working in a minor injuries unit might require courses in accident and emergency nursing while the nurse in general practice might require courses in family planning or diabetes. Educational courses usually have academic credit attached to them and these courses can be used to build towards a degree. Degree level education gives the nurse practitioner the theory required to function at an advanced level. Increasingly employers require nurse practitioners to have a degree and nurses who do not have a relevant degree may find it difficult to gain promotion.

It is currently possible to work as a clinical nurse specialist without having a degree or relevant courses in the area of practice where you work. Some prestigious hospitals and Primary Care Trusts would not consider interviewing a nurse for a clinical nurse specialist posts if the nurse did not have a degree and relevant experience and courses. For such posts some even prefer nurses who have Master's degrees. Some hospitals and Primary Care Trusts are prepared to employ nurses without such qualifications and expertise and to support these nurses in gaining them. Nurses in development posts are usually paid at lower grades than those who already have relevant qualifications and expertise. It is advisable that all nurses working at nurse specialist level have degree level qualifications and skills.

When the nurse consultant role was first introduced a Master's degree was considered to be the minimum qualification for the role. Many employers stated that they would prefer a nurse who had a doctorate (PhD or Doctor of Clinical Practice). Many employers found it difficult to recruit nurse consultants with these qualifications. Some posts are now advertised for nurses who have degrees, some for nurses who have degrees but who are studying for Master's degrees and some for those with Master's degrees who are prepared to study for a doctorate. Nurse consultants are required to have advanced clinical skills and significant expertise in their area of practice. Research carried out by King's College University London found that most nurse consultants have many years' experience in their area of practice and are qualified to Master's level.

IMPACT OF NURSE PRESCRIBING

Nurse prescribing was first suggested in 1980. In 1994 trials began on nurse prescribing and in the 1990s community nurses were able to prescribe dressings and medicines from a very limited list. Nurses working in GP practices or in hospitals were not able to prescribe. In 2003 there was a review of nurse prescribing. The government introduced a new type of prescribing known as extended and supplementary prescribing. Nurses who studied for 26 days over six months and worked with a medical prescriber could, if they completed examinations successfully, become extended and supplementary prescribers. Extended prescribing enabled nurses to prescribe from a much larger range of medicines. Supplementary prescribing enabled nurses to work in partnership with doctors using a clinical management plan to prescribe a wide range of drugs for a specific patient. There are plans to educate at least 10,000 nurse prescribers within the next few years. At the moment there are around 2,000.

This new form of prescribing gives nurses the ability to develop advanced practice. Non-prescribers are limited in their ability to treat patients. They must either use limiting protocols to supply medicines or generate a prescription and ask a doctor to sign it. Nurse prescribing enables nurses to see, diagnose and treat many patients independently.

Midwives and health visitors may also become prescribers and this will enable advanced practice to develop in these professions in the same way as it has in nursing. There are also plans to enable pharmacists and other health professionals such as chiropodists to prescribe.

INDEPENDENT PRACTICE

Nurses practising at advanced level are pioneers moving the boundaries of practice away from the old model towards independent practice. Nurses practising at advanced level are, like their medical colleagues, required to refer any patient who requires treatment that the nurse is unable to give to doctors or other professionals who are able to provide that treatment. Advanced nursing practice is developing rapidly and benefits patients who can be seen and treated without delay.

9

Working in the independent sector

The independent sector has grown in the last 25 years. Once it consisted only of a few small private hospitals and small stand-alone nursing and residential homes. Now there are more beds within the independent sector than in the NHS. The independent sector consists of private hospitals, nursing and residential homes (now known as care homes) new private walk-in centres and diagnostic treatment centres carrying out work under contract to the NHS. An estimated 100,000 nurses work in the independent sector. Many nurses who work in occupational health nursing work for private companies.

PRIVATE HOSPITALS

Private hospitals care for people who have private medical insurance. They also care for people who have decided to pay for an operation themselves. A person may have decided to pay for an operation privately because there are long NHS waiting lists. Some people choose private care because the surgery they wish to have is not available on the NHS, for example cosmetic surgery. Increasingly private hospitals also care for NHS patients who are having the costs of their treatment met by the NHS to reduce waiting lists.

Career opportunities

There are opportunities within private hospitals for nurses to gain promotion and to develop specialist practice. However, at senior level there are fewer opportunities than in the much larger NHS. Research shows that nurses who work in private hospitals are much more satisfied with their conditions than nurses who work in the NHS. Private hospitals are usually small – most have around 50 beds. In private hospitals workloads are lower and staffing is higher than in NHS hospitals.

Education and training

Private hospitals generally require nurses who are skilled in caring for people before and after surgery. A private hospital may specialise in a certain area, such as heart surgery or orthopaedic surgery, or provide care to people with a range of conditions. Private hospitals are willing to support nurses by paying course fees and giving nurses time off to attend study days and university courses in relevant subjects.

Pay and conditions

Private hospitals are not part of the NHS and are not obliged to pay NHS rates, however they do have to pay competitive rates in order to attract staff. In practice most private hospital pay rates are similar to that in the NHS. Nurses working in private hospitals often receive additional benefits such as free meals on duty and free private health care. The Royal College of Nursing produces guidance on pay rates within private hospitals. These can be downloaded from the RCN Web site (see Chapter 10).

CARE HOMES

In the past older people who required 24-hour care were cared for in NHS long-stay geriatric hospitals. In the 1980s most long-stay geriatric hospitals were closed and the government introduced funding to enable people who needed long-term care to purchase that care in a nursing or residential home. In those days there were no checks on whether an older person could benefit from rehabilitation and return home. There were no checks on what kind of care a person required. Now if a person requires 24-hour care the person is assessed to decide what level of care is required and where that care should be provided.

A patient can receive 24-hour care in his or her home, in an NHS continuing care bed or in a nursing or residential home. The decision about where care is delivered is based on the older person's needs. Nursing homes and residential homes are very different and provide different levels of care. Nursing homes must have registered nurses on duty 24 hours a day and provide nursing care. Residential care homes are not required to employ registered nurses and do not provide nursing care. If a person in a residential home has a wound that requires dressing district nurses will visit to dress the wound. In 2002 the government introduced new legislation and all homes are now registered as care homes. Some homes provide nursing care, some provide nursing and residential care and some provide residential care. Most nurses work in homes providing nursing or nursing and residential care.

The care home sector is changing. Now 25 per cent of all care homes are part of a large group, such as Westminster Health Care and 75 per cent are independently owned. Care homes that provide nursing care are becoming larger and some of the new homes have as many as 150 beds. The people cared for in care homes are much frailer and less able than before; many are admitted in the last months of life. Care homes that provide residential care are growing larger but usually have around 30 beds.

THE ROLE OF THE NURSING HOME NURSE

- Assess older people prior to admission.
- Assess nursing and care needs on admission and on an ongoing basis.
- Plan and manage care.
- Provide rehabilitation and treatment.

- Work with doctors to manage chronic diseases.
- Care for people with end stage disease.
- Provide effective palliative care.
- Work with other professionals to deliver care.
- Support older people and their families.
- Ensure that the home complies with legal standards.
- Educate nursing and care staff.
- Manage staff.
- Manage budgets.

Career opportunities

There are opportunities for nurses to work at all levels within care homes that provide nursing. There are posts for staff nurses, sisters who are often responsible for a floor or a section of a home, deputy matrons or managers who manage the home when the matron or manager is not on duty. There are also opportunities for matron managers who manage all aspects of a home including care of residents and recruitment and management of all staff employed in the home.

There are opportunities for nurses to develop specialist practice and also to teach, especially in larger homes and in homes that are part of a group. In care home groups there are opportunities for nurses to work as regional managers and to manage a group of homes. There are often excellent promotion prospects within care homes.

Education and training

There are no formal education requirements for nurses working in care homes. In practice many nurses have relevant qualifications and training. Nurses who wish to continue their education often study modules in care of older people at diploma or increasingly at degree level. Nurses also study modules in wound care, leg ulcer management, promotion of continence, palliative care and rehabilitation. These modules can be combined to make up a degree or diploma in nursing. The RCN also offers a BSc Honours degree in Gerontological Nursing. This is a distance learning course that can enable busy nurses and those with family commitments to fit degree level studies in with other responsibilities.

Care homes are required to employ large numbers of care assistants with NVQs. Many nurses within care homes study to become NVQ assessors so that they can help care assistants to obtain this qualification. Managers are now required to have experience in caring for older people and to have a recognised management qualification. This can be the NVQ level 4 registered manager's award or an alternative qualification in management.

Employers within the care home sector vary in their willingness and ability to support nurses in continuing their education. Some employers support nurses by paying course fees and giving the nurse time off to attend courses. Other employers contribute to fees and time and some employers make no contribution whatsoever. It is sensible to check an employer's policy before accepting a post.

Pay and conditions

Over 90 per cent of registered nurses who work in care homes are women and over half work part-time. Nursing homes generally offer flexible working hours and family friendly policies. Many nurses choose to work in homes that are close to home and this cuts travelling time.

Annual holidays, enhanced sickness pay and maternity leave provision are fixed in large homes that are part of groups. In smaller homes these terms and conditions are often a subject of negotiation. Working hours vary. Some homes consider a 36-hour week full-time, others consider 40 hours a week to be full-time.

Most care homes are not part of the NHS and are not obliged to pay NHS rates of pay. Pay and conditions vary enormously at all levels within care homes. The salary for a manager ranges from £45,000 for a manger of a 150-bed home to £28,000 for the manager of a 25-bed home in the London area. Some homes provide managers with a car and private medical insurance, others do not.

Salaries for deputy managers, sisters and staff nurses also vary. Some homes pay staff a premium for working unsocial hours but others do not. The RCN produces recommended salary rates for nurses working in care homes. These can be downloaded from its Web site (see Chapter 10). Agenda for Change has been designed for NHS staff but professional organisations including the RCN are calling for independent sector employers to introduce it. Agenda for Change will affect salary scales within the independent sector. The NHS and the independent sector have an ageing workforce and around 25 per cent of the nursing workforce is due to retire in the next few years. The two sectors will be competing for staff.

DIAGNOSTIC TREATMENT CENTRES

Diagnostic treatment centres are fast-track surgery centres. They will specialise in common operations for which there are currently long waiting lists. The idea is that the extra capacity in the centres will mean that patients with, for example, cataracts, can have them removed with far less delay. Currently, more than 50,000 older people are waiting over three months for cataract treatment – and one quarter of all people over 75 develop a cataract. The government has enabled NHS Trusts to set up 20 new diagnostic treatment centres. These are owned and managed by the NHS.

The government has now announced that a further 22 centres and two mobile units will be run by private companies, some of which are based overseas. These centres will be carrying out a range of surgery including complex operations such as hip and knee replacements. These centres will carry out 250,000 operations a year. There are plans to increase the number of diagnostic treatment centres to 100 by 2006.

It is not yet clear if NHS nurses will staff diagnostic treatment centres or if these centres will employ nurses directly. NHS-run diagnostic treatment centres are small, well staffed and are developing advanced practice roles for nurses.

Working in diagnostic treatment centres is, according to government policy, set to become an important part of nursing in the future.

OCCUPATIONAL HEALTH NURSING

Occupational nurses work in the NHS, in universities, in public and private companies. They work as part of a team in large organisations and as single-handed practitioners in smaller organisations. The occupational health nurse is responsible for the health and well-being of employees in the workplace. Occupational health nurses may work in large businesses and organisations or for private consultancies, as part of an occupational/environmental health and safety (EHS) team. The occupational health nurse may be the only nurse employed by a company.

THE ROLE OF THE OCCUPATIONAL HEALTH NURSE

- Screen medical questionnaires.

- Carry out pre-employment examinations, including hearing and vision screening, and health and fitness advice.

- Assess the work environment for potential health and safety problems.

- Advise the employer if a potential employee requires a medical examination.

- Design, develop and deliver new initiatives, policies and procedures on health education/promotion and accident/disease prevention.

- Conduct a range of assessments and inspections, in conjunction with regulations, such as display screen equipment (DSE), personal protective equipment (PPE) and the control of substances hazardous to health (COSHH).

■ Deliver health and safety training.

■ Provide first aid and medical treatment.

■ Advise employees on immunisation and general health.

■ Communicate safety concerns to appropriate managers.

■ Maintain employee health records, prepare accident reports.

■ Conduct accident investigation.

■ Investigate the causes of common injuries.

■ Maintain first-aid kits, order new supplies and destroy out-of-date items as necessary.

■ Assist injured employees returning to work from medical leave.

■ Monitor employee exposure to hazardous chemicals.

■ Contact doctors and/or hospitals, as necessary, to arrange further treatment.

■ Keep up to date with legal and professional changes associated with occupational health and safety.

■ Use expertise to ensure that organisations meet legislative requirements.

Career opportunities

There are opportunities for nurses to work at staff nurse, senior staff nurse, sister/charge nurse, nurse practitioner and occupational health manager level. Different organisations are able to offer different levels of post and differing opportunities for promotion. Occupational health nurses can also work in universities as nurse lecturers.

Education and training

Nurses should have an adult nursing qualification to obtain an occupational health nurse's post. Nurses who wish to progress to sister level and above are required to have qualifications in occupational health nursing. Nurses can study modules in occupational health nursing to obtain a certificate or diploma in occupational health nursing. Increasingly occupational health nursing (which is considered to be part of community nursing) is at degree level. Universities run a BSc Honours degree in Occupational Health. This is run in the same way as the district nursing and practice nursing degrees and sponsorship is available (see Chapter 7 for details). It is also possible to study occupational health nursing at Master's and doctoral level.

Pay and conditions

Occupational health nurses can work in universities as part of a team on a term-time contract. Occupational health nurses may choose to work part-time, full-time or on a sessional basis. Full-time working hours are normally 9.00 am until 5.00 pm Monday to Friday. Nurses working in the NHS will be paid on relevant Agenda for Change pay scales. These will influence pay rates in industry and other sectors.

SWAPPING SECTORS

In the past large numbers of nurses left the profession when their circumstances changed. Now nurses tend to work in different places and move from independent to NHS settings and back again. Sometimes nurses choose to work in a local care home when their children are young and then return to the NHS later. Sometimes nurses choose to take early retirement from the NHS and then decide to work on a full- or part-time basis in a private hospital, a care home or another part of the independent sector.

10

Useful addresses and information

Access to nursing courses

You can get more detailed information about access to higher education courses from your local further or adult education college or from the UCAS access courses database Internet site on:

www.ucas.ac.uk

British Council

England: The British Council, 10 Spring Gardens, London SW1A 2BN; Tel: 020 7930 8466, Fax: 020 7389 6347

Northern Ireland: The British Council, Norwich Union House, 7 Fountain Street, Belfast BT1 5EG; Tel: 028 9023 3440, Fax: 028 9024 0341

Scotland: The British Council, The Tun, 4 Jackson's Entry, Holyrood Road, Edinburgh EH8 8JP; Tel: 0131 524 5700, Fax: 0131 524 5701

Wales: 28 Park Place, Cardiff CF1 3QE; Tel: 029 20 397 346, Fax: 029 20 237 494

The British Council administers language tests. These are required for nurses who were educated in countries where English is not the first language.

For general enquiries: Tel: 0161 957 7755, Fax: 0161 957 7762, e-mail general.enquiries@britishcouncil.org

For educational enquiries: Tel: 0131 524 5770, e-mail education.enquiries@britishcouncil.org

Childcare costs

Help with childcare costs is available on a means basis to eligible parents who are NHS-funded students. Students can check their availability for help with childcare costs by calling 0845 009 2559.

Community and district nursing

Community and District Nursing Association (CDNA), Walpole House, 18–22 Bond Street, Ealing, London W5 5AA; Tel: 020 8231 0180, Web site: www.cdna.tvu.ac.uk

Course search

This Web site provides up-to-date details of pre- and post-registration nurse education programmes and study days. It contains links to the university or organisation running a particular course: www.rdlearning.org.uk

Means-tested bursaries for degree students

If you require further information contact the university you have applied to. You can also obtain information about grants in the country where you wish to study.

England: The NHS Student Grants Unit, 22 Plymouth Road, Blackpool FY3 7JS; Tel: 01253 655 655, Fax: 01253 655 660, e-mail: nhs-sgu@ukonline.co.uk

Northern Ireland: The Department of Higher and Further Education Training and Employment, Student Support Branch, 4th Floor Adelaide House, 39–49 Adelaide Street, Belfast BT2 8FD; Tel: 028 9025 7777

Scotland: The Students Awards Agency for Scotland, 3 Redheughs Rigg, South Gyle, Edinburgh EH12 9HH; Tel: 0131 4768212

Careers advice

If you wish to obtain information about nursing or midwifery careers in the UK contact the relevant organisation below.

England: NHS Careers, PO Box 376, Bristol, BS99 3EY, Tel: 0845 6060 655, e-mail: advice@nhscareers.nhs.uk, Web site: www.nhscareers.nhs.uk/careers/nursing/

Northern Ireland: Queens University Belfast, University Road, Belfast BT7 1NN; Tel: 028 9033 5081, Fax: 028 9024 7895, e-mail: admissions@qub.ac.uk, Web site: www.qub.ac.uk

University of Ulster, Jordanstown, Shore Road, Newtonabbey, Co Antrim BT37 0QB; Tel: 08 700 400 700, e-mail: online@ulst.ac.uk, Web site: www.ulst.ac.uk

Scotland: Careers Information Service, NHS Education for Scotland, 66 Rose Street, Edinburgh EH2 2NN; Tel: 0131 225 4365, Fax: 0131 225 5891, e-mail: careers@nes scot.nhs.uk, Web site: www.nes.scot.nhs.uk

Wales: Health Professions Wales, 2nd Floor, Golate House, 101 St Mary Street, Cardiff CF10 1DX; Tel: 029 2026 1400, Fax: 029 2026 1499, e-mail: info@hpw.org.uk, Web site: www.hpw.org.uk

Nursing and midwifery diploma applications

England: In England the Nursing and Midwifery Admissions Service (NMAS) processes applications for nursing diploma programmes (full-length and accelerated) and midwifery diploma programmes. The application package is available free of charge from:

NMAS, Rosehill, New Barn Lane, Cheltenham, Gloucestershire GL52 3LZ, Web site: www.nmas.ac.uk
For applications: Tel: 0870 1122200
For general enquiries: Tel: 0870 1122206

Details of vacancies are updated daily on the NMAS Web site but NMAS recommends that you telephone your chosen university to check that places are still available before applying.

Scotland: In Scotland the Central Applications for Nursing and Midwifery (CATCH) processes applications for nursing diploma programmes (full-length and accelerated) and midwifery diploma programmes. The application package is available free of charge from:

CATCH, PO Box 21, Edinburgh, EH2 2YS; Tel: 0131 220 8660 (although CATCH prefer applicants to write rather than telephone), Fax: 0131 220 8666, e-mail: careers@nes.scot.nhs.uk, Web site: www.nes.scot.nhs.uk

Nursing and midwifery degree applications

Universities and Colleges Admissions Service (UCAS) process applications for nursing and midwifery and allied professional degree programmes in England and Scotland. For further information and an application package contact:

Universities and Colleges Admissions Service (UCAS), Rosehill, New Barn Lane, Cheltenham, Gloucestershire GL52 3LZ

Nursing journals

Nursing Times
This weekly nursing journal provides news, up-to-date clinical features and a discussion board with a section for nursing students. The online jobs section can be used to find a new post, or details of training or sponsorship opportunities. www.nursingtimes.net

Nursing Standard
This is the weekly nursing journal of the RCN. It provides news and up-to-date clinical features. www.nursing-standard.co.uk

Overseas nurses

This link to the Department of Health Web site gives details of standards of supervised practice placements. www.doh.gov.uk/international-recruitment/employnurse.htm

The following link to the NMC Web site gives an up-to-date list of nursing homes approved to offer supervised practice to overseas nurses. www.nmc-uk.org/nmc/main/Overseas/Overseas11

The following links will enable you to contact NHS trusts in England, Wales, Northern Ireland and Scotland regarding supervised placements.

England: www.nhscareers.nhs.uk/nhs-knowledge_base/data/361.html

Northern Ireland: www.n-i.nhs.uk/hospitals/hospitals.html
Scotland: www.show.scot.nhs.uk/organisations/orgindex.htm
Wales: www.wales.nhs.uk/directory.cfm

Workforce development confederations

The National Workforce Group, Web site: www.national
workforce.nhs.uk

Nursing and Midwifery Council, 23 Portland Place, London
W1N 4JT; Tel: 020 7637 7181 (general number); Web site:
www.nmc-uk.org.uk. Registration hotline for nurses
registered in UK: 020 7333 3333. Registration hotline for
nurses applying for registration who were not educated in the
EU: 020 7333 6600. The NMC maintains a register of all
practising midwives, nurses and health visitors. It is a
statutory body and is there to protect the public hence it has a
role in investigating allegations of professional misconduct
and negligent practice.

The Royal College of Midwives, 15 Mansfield St, London
W1G 9NH.

The Royal College of Midwives exists to protect the
professional interests of midwives and to advance the art and
science of midwifery.

The Royal College of Nursing, 20 Cavendish Square, London
W1G 0RN; Tel: 020 7409 3333, Web site: www.rcn.org.uk

RCN Northern Ireland, 17 Windsor Avenue, Belfast, BT9 6EE;
Tel: 028 9066 8236, e-mail: ni.board@rcn.org.uk

RCN Scotland, 42 South Oswald Road, Edinburgh EH9 2HH;
Tel: 0131 622 1010, e-mail: scottish.board@rcn.org.uk

RCN Wales, Ty Maeth, King George V Drive East, Cardiff
CF14 4XZ; Tel: 029 2075 1373, e-mail: welsh.board@rcn.org.uk

The Royal College of Nursing is the world's largest trade
union. It has 370,000 members. It provides support to nurses
who have problems in work and works to advance the art and
science of nursing. The RCN has branches across all of the UK
regions, the main branches are given above.

Further reading from Kogan Page

For these and further titles visit www.kogan-page.co.uk.

CAREERS

Clabby, K (2004) *Careers and Jobs in the Police Service*

Kent, S (2004) *Careers and Jobs in the Media*

Krechowiecka, I (2004) *The A–Z of Careers and Jobs*, 11th edn

Reilly Collins, V (2004) *Careers and Jobs in Travel and Tourism*

Yardley, D (2004) *Careers and Jobs in IT*

TESTING

Barrett, J (2004) *Aptitude, Personality and Motivation Tests*

Barrett, J (2003) *The Aptitude Test Workbook*

Carter, P (2004) *IQ and Psychometric Tests*

Russell, K and Carter, P *(2003) The Times Book of IQ Tests –
Book 3*

Smith, H (2003) *How to Pass Numerical Reasoning Tests*

JOB SEARCH

Williams, L (2004) *Readymade CVs*, 3rd edn

Williams, L (2004) *Readymade Job Search Letters*, 3rd edn

Yate, M (2001) *Great Answers to Tough Interview Questions*, 5th edn

Appendix

NUMERACY TESTS

There are a number of resources available to help health care professionals develop numeracy skills. The University of the West of England's Faculty of Health and Social Care has produced an excellent learning resource which enables applicants to test their skills. The Faculty has kindly permitted reproduction of a small sample of its support material. To find its complete numeracy skills support material go to http://learntec.uwe.ac.uk/numeracy/index.asp

Decimals

When working with multi-digit numbers such as 435, the three numbers have quite different values. 435 is read as four hundred and thirty-five: the digit 4 counts hundreds, the digit 3 counts tens and the digit 5 counts units.

All money can be written in decimal form. £20 can be written as £20.00 with a decimal point separating the pounds and pence. The part of the number after the decimal point records parts of wholes.

Subtract the following:

1. $1-0.8 =$
2. $1-0.4 =$
3. $1-0.76 =$
4. $1-0.75 =$
5. $1-0.18 =$
6. $1-0.51 =$

Multiply the following:

1.   2.14 x 10 =
2.   7.82 x 100 =
3.   5.49 x 10 =
4.   0.083 x 10 =
5.   742 x 100 =
6.   769 x 10 =

Add the following. You may use a calculator if you wish.

1.   9.15 + 6.97 + 8.5 + 0.354 =
2.   6.33 + 93.8 + 5.78 + 8.17 + 4.27 =
3.   2.86 + 2.17 + 2.76 + 9.31 =
4.   75.2 + 9.4 + 1.53 + 1.51 =
5.   4.31 + 0.814 + 68.6 + 4.9 =

Divide the following:

1.   29.2 ÷ 100 =
2.   949 ÷ 10 =
3.   61÷ 1000 =
4.   9.96 ÷ 100 =
5.   19 ÷ 10 =
6.   1.19 ÷ 10 =

Percentages

Percentage is a convenient method of representing the part of a whole expressed in hundredths. Per cent means per hundred and is expressed as the symbol %. This symbol means 'divided by 100'.

Find the following amounts. Make sure that you use the correct units.

1.   70% of 80 =
2.   70% of 400 =
3.   70% of 50 =
4.   35% of £700 =
5.   35% of £20 –
6.   35% of £900 =
7.   135% of 30 kg =
8.   135% of £40 =
9.   135% of £800 =

10. 10% of 200 =
11. 10% of 50 =
12. 10% of 800 =
13. 5% of 30 kg =
14. 5% of 600 ml =
15. 5% of 400 g =
16. 105% of 10 kg =
17. 105% of 60 g =
18. 105% of 500 g =
19. 70% of 60 =
20. 70% of 600 =
21. 70% of 40 =
22. 35% of £1000 =
23. 35% of 80 kg =
24. 35% of 300 g =
25. 135% of 700 ml =
26. 135% of 30 g =
27. 135% of 50 ml =
28. 70% of 90 =
29. 70% of 400 =
30. 70% of 80 =
31. 35% of 40 ml =
32. 35% of 800 ml =
33. 35% of 300 g =
34. 135% of 200 kg =
35. 135% of 500 g =
36. 135% of £600 =

Ratios

Ratios are used to compare two or more quantities. A ratio shows how many times bigger one quantity is than another.

Express the following ratios in their simplest terms.

1. 80 : 90 =
2. 2 : 4 =
3. 8 : 16 =
4. 12 : 21 =
5. 18 : 9 =
6. 5 : 35

7. $9 : 9 =$
8. $21 : 3 =$
9. $5 : 25 =$
10. $9 : 45 =$
11. $54 : 48 =$
12. $6 : 16 =$
13. $5 : 15 =$
14. $20 : 35$
15. $4 : 8 =$
16. $6 : 6 =$
17. $2 : 24 =$
18. $36 : 27 =$
19. $56 : 8 =$
20. $9 : 9 =$
21. $1 : 1 =$
22. $3 : 7 =$
23. $27 : 45 =$
24. $10 : 6 =$
25. $2 : 6 =$
26. $3 : 8 =$
27. $32 : 72 =$
28. $48 : 56 =$
29. $24 : 18 =$
30. $54 : 6 =$
31. $16 : 20 =$
32. $4 : 2 =$
33. $9 : 7 =$
34. $7 : 7 =$
35. $15 : 27 =$
36. $4 : 4 =$
37. $16 : 18 =$
38. $28 : 21 =$
39. $35 : 25 =$
40. $9 : 12 =$

Writing fractions as decimals

Writing the fraction 4 over 10, $\frac{4}{10}$ is simply another way of writing 4 divided by 10.

$$\frac{4}{10} = 4 \div 10 = 0.4$$

1. $\frac{6}{10} =$

2. $\frac{6}{100} =$

3. $\frac{14}{100} =$

4. $\frac{76}{100} =$

5. $\frac{979}{1000} =$

6. $\frac{850}{1000} =$

7. $\frac{1}{10} =$

8. $\frac{2}{10} =$

9. $\frac{91}{100} =$

10. $\frac{79}{100} =$

11. $\frac{275}{1000} =$

12. $\frac{450}{1000} =$

13. $\frac{56.6}{100} =$

14. $\frac{7.93}{1000} =$

15. $\frac{78}{100} =$

ANSWERS

Subtractions

1. 0.2
2. 0.6
3. 0.24
4. 0.25
5. 0.82
6. 0.49

Multiplication

1. 21.4
2. 782
3. 54.9
4. 0.83
5. 74200
6. 7690

Addition

1. 24.974
2. 118.35
3. 17.1
4. 87.64
5. 78.624

Division

1. 0.292
2. 94.9
3. 0.061
4. 0.0996
5. 1.9
6. 0.119

Percentages

1. 56
2. 280
3. 35

4. £245
5. £7.00
6. £315
7. 40.5 kg
8. £54.00
9. £1080
10. 20
11. 5
12. 80
13. 1.5 kg
14. 30 ml
15. 20 g
16. 10.5 kg
17. 63 g
18. 525 g
19. 42
20. 420
21. 28
22. £350
23. 28 kg
24. 105 g
25. 945 ml
26. 40.5 g
27. 67.5 ml
28. 63
29. 280
30. 56
31. 14 ml
32. 280 ml
33. 105 g
34. 270 kg
35. 675 g
36. £810

Ratios

1. 8 : 9
2. 1 : 2
3. 1 : 2
4. 4 : 7

5. 2 : 1
6. 1 : 7
7. 1 : 1
8. 7 : 1
9. 1 : 5
10. 1 : 5
11. 9 : 8
12. 3 : 8
13. 1 : 3
14. 4 : 7
15. 1 : 2
16. 1 : 1
17. 1 : 12
18. 4 : 3
19. 7 : 1
20. 1 : 1
21. 1 : 1
22. 3 : 7
23. 3 : 5
24. 5 : 3
25. 1 : 3
26. 3 : 8
27. 4 : 9
28. 6 : 7
29. 4 : 3
30. 9 : 1
31. 4 : 5
32. 2 : 1
33. 9 : 7
34. 1 : 1
35. 5 : 9
36. 1 : 1
37. 8 : 9
38. 4 : 3
39. 7 : 5
40. 3 : 4

Writing fractions as decimals

1. 0.6
2. 0.06
3. 0.14
4. 0.76
5. 0.979
6. 0.85
7. 0.1
8. 0.2
9. 0.91
10. 0.79
11. 0.275
12. 0.45
13. 0.566
14. 0.00793
15. 0.78

Index

INDEX OF ADVERTISERS